LIBRARY

Demos is ... for return on or before the last date

to ... ... societies.
fac ... It ... ... cal and practical
to help ... ... and to
improve the ... ... ebate.
Demos publishes boo... ... rnal
and undertakes substantia... ... policy-
oriented research projects. Demos ... registered charity.

In all its work Demos brings together people from
a wide range of backgrounds in business, academia,
government, the voluntary sector and the media to
share and cross-fertilise ideas and experiences.

For further information and
subscri ion details please ... to:
Demo
9 Bri ell Place
Lond 4V 6A
Tele 71 9
Fac
ema

The Other Invisible Hand: Remaking charity for the 21st century

Geoff Mulgan and Charles Landry

DEM⊚S

First published in 1995 by
Demos
9 Bridewell Place
London EC4V 6AP
Telephone: 0171 353 4479
Facsimile: 0171 353 4481
© Demos 1995

Paper No. 15
ISBN 1 898309 81 7
Printed in Great Britain by
EG Bond
Designed by Esterson Lackersteen
Thanks to Adrian Taylor

Contents

Acknowledgements

This report would not have been possible without the kind support of the Charities Aid Foundation and the Joseph Rowntree Foundation, and in particular the active involvement of Michael Brophy and Richard Best.

We would also like to acknowledge the support of the following members of the advisory group who have helped with the project: Cathy Ashton, Richard Best from the Joseph Rowntree Foundation, Michael Brophy and Simon Hebditch from CAF, Alan Howarth MP, Melinda Letts, Director, National Asthma Campaign, John Plummer, Usha Prashar, Bill Solesbury of the ESRC, Katrin Tilley of Charity Projects, Patrick Wright and Henry Drucker of Oxford Philanthropic.

Paul Hoggett of the University of The West of England, Russell Sparkes of the UK Social Investment Forum, John Griffiths and Lester Salamon of Johns Hopkins University contributed extremely valuable working papers on which we have drawn substantially for this report (these are listed at the back). We have also received invaluable help throughout the project from Nicholas Deakin, Stephen Lea, Michael Norton, Stephen Thake, Diana Leat, Marilyn Taylor, Alun Michael MP, Pat Conaty and Perri 6, who is now research director at Demos and editor of *Non-Profit Studies*.

Finally the report has depended on hundreds of people up and down the country who have attended seminars and spared time to talk to us during the course of the project.

The need for a new settlement: summary and introduction

Britain is not a nation at ease with itself. In almost every field policy-makers are struggling with intractable problems that are not responding to orthodox solutions. The problems of drugs, housing, ill health, unemployment, pollution, racial tension and urban decay are only the most visible.

For much of this century, government might have been expected to offer solutions to these problems. But today, it often has neither the will nor the means. In the 19th century traditional charities, too, might have been expected to fill the gap. But their capacities are too limited, and their structures too antiquated to be effective or legitimate.

In this report we argue that the priority now is to find new ways of mobilising and channelling voluntary energies - the energy to give, to help, to create and to change - in ways that fit with the culture and norms of today. The approach is strikingly different to that of the government, whose main initiative of recent years has been the National Lottery, generating large sums of money under central control, and probably leading to a net decline in money available for charitable organisations. And it represents a strikingly different

approach to those who focus solely on tax and
redistribution as the way to solve social problems.

At the core of the analysis is the belief that all modern
societies depend on two invisible hands. One is the
invisible hand of self-interest that works through the
market to promote economic prosperity. The other is the
invisible hand of generosity, help and moral commitment
that sustains a sense of community and mutual
responsibility. In recent years this second invisible hand
has been relatively ignored. Britain and other western
societies have proven much better at managing material
advancement and outlets for self-interest, and at
organising professional service delivery, than they have
been at providing outlets and encouragements for moral
impulses. Yet experience has shown that without the
effective organisation of helping behaviour societies
become diminished. The quality of life, the delivery of
services, the sense of community: all suffer.

But it is neither possible nor desirable to return to
older models. The heritage of charity, one of the main
vehicles by which the other invisible hand is organised, is
increasingly out of step with modern society. The main
laws and concepts are centuries old and are now too
paternalistic, inflexible, too inappropriate to economic
activity and at odds with a democratic culture.

Yet despite the anachronism of much charity, and
despite the relative myopia of politics, we argue that there
are good reasons for believing that the next century could
bring a renaissance of the civic - of people's ethical
connections to each other and to larger purposes. This
may seem a surprising claim. In most western societies
people's sense of civic attachment seems to have grown
weak. There is a widespread sense of loss of community in
much of the Western world, and a loss of faith in
institutions. The conditions for traditional communities -
deference, social homogeneity, immobility - have
disappeared.

Today every place is connected to many others by
media, telecommunications and travel; by people's many

attachments; by the wider spread of interdependence which means that few depend any more on their close family or neighbours. Only 11.2% of city dwellers feel there is a sense of community where they live, and barely a quarter know their neighbours well. Moreover in other respects society has become disconnected and dislocated with the decline of great political blocs and churches. Many of the old attachments have gone: between 1971 and 1992, for example, membership of the St Johns Ambulance brigade fell 45%, the Women's Institute 33.3%, the Girl Guides 29% and the Boy Scouts 11.2%.[1] Church going has declined by 1.5 million in the last 15 years.

Yet it is hard not to be struck by the strength of the countervailing forces: the urge to belong, to participate and to achieve change; the burgeoning non-profit sectors and associations across the world; the fact that relative prosperity releases people to cultivate their values and enthusiasms. Over the last decade, for example, the memberships of Friends of the Earth and Greenpeace have grown from 50,000 to over 550,000. Income for organizations such as Save the Children, Oxfam or the RSPCA has roughly tripled over the same period. Innovative forms of fundraising like Live Aid or Comic Relief have both tapped people's emotions and shown that sympathy and a willingness to help is present when approached in the right way. The charitable impulse remains, but its forms have changed.

This, we argue, is the foundation on which we need to build. While the report concentrates on the formally defined charitable and voluntary sector, its scope is broader. It looks at the deeper motivations that encourage voluntary and charitable action in the first place. It deliberately directs attention away from the roles of service delivery and the contract culture which have dominated debate in the voluntary sector in recent years, important though they are, and looks instead at the means to realise a more connected society.

The starting point for policy, we argue, is the recognition that ethical impulses are part of human nature. If markets depend on material self-interests, governments on coercion, the base of the non-profit sector is moral commitment. These commitments will not always be consistent. Indeed it is the nature of ethics that they often clash. But a more ethically engaged and literate society will tend to make for a better quality of life, in its widest sense, and for both givers and receivers.

From 1601 to 2001

The space for voluntary action has been repeatedly redefined since 1601 when the basic legal concepts of charity came into being. In this century the major new settlements took place after 1945, when charity was pushed to the margins as the state rolled forward, and after 1979 as the voluntary sector was brought in as a contractor for services.

Why is there a need for a new settlement, perhaps one timed to coincide with the 400th anniversary of 1601? The first reason is that the sector has become differentiated. Dozens of large service providing organisations have grown up, primarily dependent on government contracts (and not that dissimilar from for-profit organisations either in terms of staff motivation or the responsiveness of management). New generations of campaigning organisations have come into being, as well as thousands of self-help organisations. The result, as we shall see, is that almost all of the old definitions are straining at the limits: there are charities that are really service providers, campaigns dressed up as educational bodies, mutual aid organisations having to pretend that they are not in order to qualify for charitable status. As a consequence almost all of the dominant policy moves of the last couple of decades have proved at best problematic (the rise of contracting), at worst futile (tax reliefs). But there are also other factors demanding a fresh perspective. One is the marked internationalisation of the sector. The overseas aid charities have been amongst the most successful in recent years. Across the world, non-government organisations have steadily grown in stature, with a leading role around development agencies, in the Rio conference and in initiatives like Local Agenda 21. Within Europe, housing associations are beginning to operate across borders, while community bodies are learning to collaborate to qualify for the European Union funds. Umbrella bodies are thinking internationally - with the Charity Knowhow Fund, the international telethon, the Charity Aid Foundation's work in the USA and Russia, and the work of the Charity Commission in Eastern Europe. More than ever ideas are spreading globally - ideas like the contracting models that rapidly spread from American states like Massachussetts into the UK public sector, or the Foyer concept that has been imported from France. And perhaps of most significance for the long-term, an embryonic global civil society is taking form around issues like the environment, human, or women's rights, just as it has long existed around the major religions.

Another driver of change is belief and motivation. Public values are changing profoundly and moving further away from the old Christian religious roots of charity and their ideas of sacrifice and duty. Instead the dominant values increasingly stress self-responsibility, commitment, integrity as well as the pleasure to be had from engaging in voluntary action. They are evolving around a new everyday language of commitment that is far more alive than the atrophied language of the public, social, and civic. All of these changes are taking place at an extraordinary pace. They have fuelled a lively debate that has been helped by reports such as the Centris study for the Home Office, the University of Kent Study and the current NCVO Commission on the future of the voluntary sector. These are confirming that the sector, if it can justifiably be called one, remains defined legally by a ragbag of outdated rules and definitions, by tax privileges that are often inappropriate, and by rules of governance that are at best ill-defined and at worst paternalistic.

Achieving a new fiscal and legal framework for voluntary action will not be easy. There are innumerable details and complexities involved. But any government which achieves it will be chiming in with a powerful popular mood for new means of belonging and new ways to reconnect people to their society and communities. It will also be in tune with a global shift towards new forms of association and self-reliance in place of the bureaucratic state and big business.

Amongst dozens of recommendations, this report sets out some of the elements. It argues for:

● A simplified set of core legal principles from which organisations should be able to choose - balancing incentives for participants, liability and risk-taking, and accountability. These should be developed to replace the cumbersome and anachronistic legal forms, with often unlimited liability, through which most voluntary activity now has to operate.

● The development of new models of public funding, involving a partnership between government and charities, linked to more sophisticated measures of success, including subjective and qualitative indicators that involve the public in their definition.

● Tax benefits to be given to activities commonly defined as public goods rather than specific organizational forms such as charities.

● New financial mechanisms to direct money to social goals: in particular a system of voluntary taxation using the Inland Revenue for taxpayers to earmark money to charitable activity.

● New support for charitable investments, loans, bonds and guarantees; and a new set of institutions including a Charity Bank, all to provide new outlets for individual generosity.

● Removing the remaining restrictions on free speech for charities, to enable them to play a full part in political life.

● An 'Investors in the Community' kitemark for companies involved in community activities, so as to promote responsible business involvement in community activities.

● A new CONNECT scheme for community service, for the unemployed and others, whereby volunteer time is exchanged for public funding in order to create useful work and participation in society.

● A shift in public funding to deliberately encourage innovation and experiment, with a fixed percentage of non-profit organisation funding (initially 0.5%) for overt 'risk' funding.

These steps we argue would be useful starting points. They would significantly change the operating environment for voluntary action. But what we are driving at is also something less easily defined: a change in culture towards a more engaged and committed society.

The role of ethics and a wider sense of self-interest

If you explore any city, town or neighbourhood in Britain, you soon find an extraordinary undergrowth of voluntary action. Amateurs, enthusiasts and the committed join together in self-help groups, clubs, associations and federations, in a myriad of activities stretching from health, social welfare, leisure, recreation, education, to community development and conservation. In Kingswood a suburban area east of Bristol, for example, a recent survey found 315 voluntary leisure groups. The local authority was aware of only 80. Together these organisations form a dense web, often unseen, often unrecognised or appreciated, based on a commitment to voluntary action. They embody what the ancient world called the 'vita activa,' the engaged public life.

Why do people take part? Why do they give time to voluntary enthusiasms or great causes? And what makes for sustained commitment to voluntary action? There is a wide range of answers. In part local commitment is an important factor, and tends to be stronger in the coastal areas of Britain (Tyne and Wear, Humberside, Merseyside) and weakest in the commuter belts of the Southeast and West Midlands. Another is the presence of non-employed women who have always been the stalwarts of local charity. A third is the direct local influence of charismatic individuals, the social entrepreneurs who often create and drive voluntary organisations. But much of the answer, we argue, is less specific than this. It lies as much in human nature as in religious or other external pressures.

This other nature is the base for what we describe as the other invisible hand. The Western world has grown up with the idea of an invisible hand in economics. In the late 18th century Adam Smith demonstrated that if laws and government provided rewards for the pursuit of self-interest, all would benefit. With stable currencies and properly conceived property rights, the economy could be left to organise itself, drawing, as it were, on underlying, and endlessly renewable, properties of human nature. It was a vision of a self-organising system that was radically different from the hierarchical feudal models that preceded it. Today, as a result, we have a panoply of measures designed to steer and encourage that invisible hand. Tax incentives, company laws, accounting rules and the like are all shaped to encourage competitive material self-interest to flower.

But experience has shown that societies cannot live by this kind of self-interest alone. Smith himself acknowledged in *The Theory of Moral Sentiment* that people also need to be bound by other values: sympathy, compassion and fellow feeling. And many have acknowledged that the narrow view of self-interest to be found in much of the economics that has followed Smith bears only a limited relationship to the reality of human motivations and satisfaction.

But in Adam Smith's day, and in the time of the 19th and early 20th century philosophers, relatively little was known about the precise details of human nature, and thus about how to ground or weight these various motives and sentiments. It was possible to have endless debates about whether people are 'really' selfish or co-operative, private or social. For some, the role of government and religion was to suppress malign animal instincts, while for others the innate goodness of human nature simply needed to be released and utopia would follow.

Today, by contrast, we are in a better position to draw on the evidence of psychology and anthropology, history and biology, to make some tentative judgements, not only about human nature but also about fulfilment, and the ways in which policies relate to them.

Are ethics innate?
In the past what was thought good about humans and their actions was often ascribed to learning and what was bad ascribed to instinct. Martin Luther, for example, stated that man is wicked by nature, a slave of base passions and corrupt reason. Thomas Hobbes wrote that 'every man is enemy to every man'. For centuries, many have argued that only moral codes, reinforced by religion or laws, can curtail these base, self-interested, potentially destructive instincts. According to this view charity is one of many imposed duties: a necessary burden of tradition that goes against the instinct to selfish behaviour. This view has a modern equivalent. According to many pessimists we have today lost precisely these bearings and religious commitments, and are governed only by immediate impulses or calculating self-interest. As James Q. Wilson summarised this view, 'God is dead or silent, reason suspect or defective, nature meaningless or hostile. As a result we are left adrift on an uncharted sea, left to find moral bearings with no compass or pole star, and so able to do no more than utter personal preferences, bow to historical necessity or social conventions'.[2]

This view has profound implications - it means that no law has any real foundation in a widely shared sense of innate justice, and thus that the moral codes and the laws that embody them are nothing more than expressions of the interests of those with power. It suggests that attempts to foster a willingness to help are futile unless backed by some new authority and that even actions which appear generous turn out to be solely self-interested.

Yet this view is being challenged. And the ways in which it is being rethought have profound implications for how we think about charity and helping behaviour. The most important source is the emerging science of evolutionary psychology, whose proponents argue that morality, like language, has a basis in human biology. Various moral predispositions, they argue, evolved because of their evolutionary advantages and are now universal: to be found in every culture, and in societies throughout history. These predispositions include kinship and reciprocal altruism, sociability, fairness, sympathy, self-control, duty.

Such predispositions are everyday. They can be observed in a random example of three reports in the London *Evening Standard* of the 25th April 1995. Miep Gies, who hid Anne Frank and her family in her attic and was in London to commemorate the 50th anniversary of her death said: 'I only did my human duty, helping people who needed help - no more'. John Hoddinott, the Chief Constable of Hampshire, who refused to sign the new Home-Office inspired fixed-term appointment because it contained an element of performance related pay, even though it would give him a salary increase of £12,000, was reported as saying 'I joined the police out of a sense of public service..... recognising the financial disadvantage. The notion that I will work harder or more effectively, because of performance related pay is absurd and objectionable, if not insulting.' Finally on the business page there was an article headlined 'To be green is becoming better for you.......Good for career, company and country', which reported that 'Managers who rise up the ladder are those who are in touch with the trends and expectations of customers and that includes being environmentally aware'.

Some would explain each of these examples in terms of culture.[3] But the implication of the work of people like Robert Wright,[4] Leda Cosmides[5] and James Q. Wilson[6] is that however important culture may be the roots of ethical behaviour lie deeper, in a set of moral senses. Perhaps the most important is natural sociability: scores of studies have shown that new-borns are sociable before they have even learnt to be sociable, just as they can communicate far better than would be the case if they simply learnt from their parents. This natural sociability motivates people to belong, and to be accepted, and this is the first motive that later encourages people to take part in projects and causes.

In the same way few can avoid sympathy - our sense of another person's feelings, which manifests itself in actions like taking in a Romanian orphan or giving to a homeless person on the street. Simply for survival reasons most people wish to encourage in each other the sentiment of sympathy, and this in turn is affirmed by rewarding its display. Other crucial moral senses include the sense of duty (which often seems to derive from attachments) and the sense of fairness, which, like the other senses, can be found in an extraordinarily wide range of cultures, and which can also be observed in toddlers (and indeed in public anxieties over such things as executive pay).

Reciprocal altruism
Perhaps the key concept is reciprocal altruism. For evolutionary biologists it is paradoxical that willingness to help occurs even though it would appear to reduce reproductive fitness. Reciprocal altruism describes the tendency to undertake altruistic acts such as helping non-relatives or caring for adopted children, in order to impress upon others our dependability and hence to increase our chances of having profitable exchanges with others. Having a reputation for doing one's duty and living up to expectations will enhance our own opportunities. In this and other cases moral behaviour is more common, as Wilson puts it, 'When utility conspires with duty; the strongest moral codes are those that combine advantage and obligation,'[7] such as when elderly people willingly pay for the education of the young as it is

they who will pay their future pensions. This norm of reciprocity appears to be universal.

Self-interest and the moral senses
The various predispositions or moral senses are not, of course, always dominant. They are precarious; such other-regarding sentiments are not the sole determinants of action - circumstance, the rewards, rituals and penalties of daily life - constrain or subvert the operation of our moral intuitions. To say people have a moral sense is not to say they are innately good. Nor is it to say that we are all in possession of moral absolutes and act upon them. The other-regarding moral senses must compete with other instincts that are also natural to humans - the desire to survive, have sex or accumulate power.

But the key point is that the moral senses or dispositions, like the dispositions with which they must compete, have an adaptive value; if they did not, natural selection would have soon eliminated them and favoured only those with the capacity for ruthless plundering, immediate gratifications or a disinclination to share.[8]

This is, of course, only a starting point. Few of us are slaves to our genes. Each individual, each group and each society has to choose whether to cultivate ethical behaviour or whether to follow a narrower view of what life is for.

But this argument provides an important first base. It explains why ethical behaviour is present in everything from the small community involvements of a highly commercial manufacturing firm to the purely altruistic work of a Church mission, and in a vast range of different activities in between, such as the varied landscape of ethical investment, gifts, professional non-profits, in which many different motivations of self-interest, pay, generosity and pure curiosity combine. And whereas the law seeks to give sharp definition to the difference between organisations based on profit and those based on altruism, the implication of this argument is that human motivations will rarely divide so neatly.

Indeed, the virtue of many of the evolutionary arguments is that they confirm our observation that there is no clear boundary between self-interest and what might be termed other-directed behaviour. Little of what takes place in the voluntary sector is altruistic in any clear sense. Altruism implies sacrifice or a burden. But most contemporary evidence suggests something much more akin to a reciprocal relationship, in which givers get a great deal back. Perhaps the best evidence for this was a recent survey by Michael Argyle, Professor of Psychology at Oxford University, on the sources of joy for people in modern Britain.

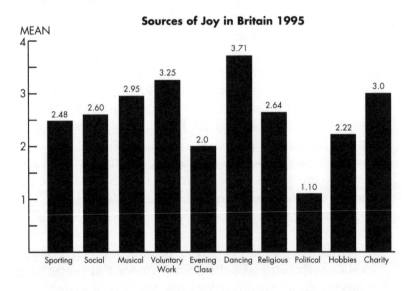

Sources of Joy in Britain 1995

Perhaps not surprisingly, dancing comes top. Equally unsurprisingly perhaps, politics comes bottom. But few would have forecast that charity and voluntary activity would actually come higher than sports and music. It is evidence of this kind that puts paid to the old idea of charity as a necessary duty, and shows instead that an ethical and connected life is in tune with our underlying nature, a rational pursuit of fulfilling exchanges. It illuminates, too, an older idea of happiness. When

Jefferson wrote in the American Declaration of Independence that the 'pursuit of happiness' was an inalienable right, he had in mind a more public notion of happiness than we have today, a satisfaction with the performance of the society, the well-being of the community.[9] The fact that today, still, our joy comes from engagement as much as from private pleasures suggests that this insight has lost none of its relevance.[10]

Institutional expressions

The charity heritage

The religious connection

Historically the manifestations of moral and ethical senses have been shaped by prevailing cultures. In medieval times in the West charity was very much the preserve of the church and its various organs, primarily the monasteries and hospitals. The word 'caritas', referring to the duty of care, was a central concept in Christian theology. But charity has never been adequately contained by this religious heritage. Instead political definitions and priorities have also repeatedly intervened. The famous preamble of 1601, which first established the modern principles of charity law, was predominantly secular in inspiration, and set out a series of public policy challenges fit for an era of social fragmentation, growing inequality and joblessness. Its aim was to draw on the social and moral energy of the new urban middle classes to help tackle everything from the peace dividend to public works.

Subsequently, the religious element has waxed and waned. Much of what qualifies for charity today - whether the public schools or high art - bears no relation to the ideas of St Paul or St Thomas Aquinas. It might fit with the moral dispositions towards sociability and helping children, but not with stricter notions of altruism and helping behaviour. Indeed the impulse to sociability may override other moral senses, so people may give to friends or institutions they already support like the opera house or the upkeep of an old building, rather than to strangers or those in more desperate need. By contrast, most public opinion still thinks of charity in Christian terms - meeting the needs of the poor and powerless.

Charity has also not always been regarded as an unalloyed blessing. With the rise of a democratic culture in the 19th century it was no longer seen as inherently benign; it could just as easily be seen as demeaning, unequal and disempowering. The structures of charitable organisation were criticised for fostering dependency, while the pattern of charity provision was seen as parochial, inefficient and uneven providing a hospital here or an educational institution there but not reflecting national patterns of need. Some, like Lester Salamon in the US, would argue that this is still the case. But it was the power relationship at the heart of charity that most concerned the critics. Beveridge, for example, criticised philanthropy for its association with business, profit and the largesse of the powerful, contrasting it with the liberating power of mutual aid.

The state intervenes
The failure of charity to cope with the problems thrown up by industrial society justified the rapid extension of the state's role in welfare. Government, it was argued, could provide more consistent, comprehensive provision, based on the rights of the receiver and compulsory taxation rather than the goodwill of the giver. The late Victorian view that, in Jose Harris' words, 'Moral character, active citizenship and 'public spirit' were the indispensable building blocks of a well-ordered society and a virtuous state'[11] came to seem anachronistic. Between 1945 and 1951 most of health and education were taken into government so that, like welfare, they

could be funded out of progressive taxation without the stigma of the Poor Law. Charity became, in Frank Prochaska's words the 'junior partner in the welfare firm'.[12] At the same time the moral and ethical impulse that was so crucial to 19th century politics, charity and mutual aid activities was lost, replaced instead by more technical discussions of distribution or rights.

The result of this shift was to sharply increase the overall volume of redistribution. Redistribution through charity was in fact never very large in monetary terms. Monies paid from the state through taxation and distributed in benefits now account for over 25% of GDP compared to less than 1% for transfers through charity. But this apparent rise in collective generosity was never ethically unambiguous. Today, ironically, the welfare state suffers from the same charge of creating dependency as 19th century charity. It is seen not so much as immoral as amoral and disempowering. Partly this is an effect of the forms the state has taken. While in the 19th century new forms of organisation were invented to counteract dependency, such as the co-operative movement, or mutual and friendly societies, government until recently preferred hierarchical, administrative solutions. Services were predominantly delivered by professionals, without the active engagement of beneficiaries, and most funding of voluntary bodies preferred large-scale service providers over community organisations. Although two-thirds of registered charities have incomes less than £10,000, in the words of Gabriel Chanan of the Community Development Foundation 'only a tiny trickle' of public funding reaches down to independent community groups. In other words, as the state took on the characteristic organisational forms of the industrial age, in large scale hierarchical structures, the parallel tradition of voluntary collective action, seemed to wane.

During the last two decades, however, there has been a reappraisal. In many different quarters there has been a questioning of the virtues of large scale; of excessive hierarchy; of administrative standardisation; and indeed of professional autonomy. With this reappraisal, which has involved participants from the radical free market right to the green left, has come the beginnings of a rather different view of the characteristics of good organisations and good government, with emphases on choice and power, on small scale community-based structures, on clearly defined values, and on much more sharing of information and judgement between providers and beneficiaries.

The idea of charity under attack
But despite the disenchantment with big government, the pendulum has not swung back to an unthinking admiration of charity and voluntary action. Nor is this just a result of (often misinformed) public scepticism about high administration and marketing costs or the occasional fraud. Instead the issue goes deeper. There is an underlying unease about the concept of charity itself. Some of that unease can be discerned in the phrase 'cold as charity', an interesting reverse of the original meaning which reflects the manners of many older charitable institutions. Raymond Williams wrote that 'it is not surprising that the word which was once the most general expression of love and care for others has become so compromised that modern governments have to advertise welfare benefits as 'not charity but a right'.'[13]

Many of the words around charity have also changed their meaning. 'Do-gooder' has become a word of abuse and suspicion, as has 'professional do-gooder', which implies someone who is interfering rather than enabling. The changing nuances of the word 'worthy' are also instructive, as is the distinction between 'moral' and 'moralistic'. Much the same linguistic atrophy has affected a cluster of other words: public, civic, social even community (which is used to describe everything from punishments - 'community service' - to taxes - 'the community charge'). Where one group of words has been tarnished by its association with an arrogant paternalism, the second set have suffered from their cooption by governments, and thus their identification with bureaucracy.

Is there a coherent sector?
But even if this was not the case, the word 'charity' would still be problematic. For charities (and voluntary organisations) no longer constitute a sector in any coherent sense, even though bodies like the NCVO seek to represent it as such. The sheer diversity of activity, range of structures, organisational type and scale makes it difficult even to discuss them in one breath. At one extreme there is the Royal Opera House, still essentially a bastion of privilege focused on a narrow audience, the National Trust, a multi-million pound business, or the WVRS, its head appointed by government, and its core resource around 140,000 volunteers. These are highly professional organisations with well paid staff. At the other extreme there are small self-help groups, scouts, church or sports clubs operating on a purely voluntary basis with little or no resources. In between there is a mass of research institutes, schools, museums or housing projects, and a wide range of charity support organisations such as Community Computing Network, local agencies like the Nottingham Self-Help team (which backs self-help groups), through to the charity NDL's market research services.

This sheer diversity sometimes contributes to the public's confusion, and is certainly exacerbated by the proliferation of new bodies - like TECs or Hospital Trusts - operating in the grey area between government, business and charity. But one of the biggest problems is surely that so many charities are not concerned with the poor, but rather with servicing the rich: not only through providing services in the arts and education, but also in providing a sphere of recreational dinners and other events. For them the disposition towards sociability seems to outweigh any wider sympathy or sense of fairness. In a more limited way the same problem is visible amongst service providing charities (such as housing associations or schools), which, under the pressures of a contracting culture, often tend to move upmarket.

Conversely many organisations which are not charities seem just as committed to core charitable values. This is true of some non-charitable religious organisations, of alternative trading companies, food and worker co-ops, self-help health groups, artistic and political organisations, and intentional communities, such as communes. Firms like Traidcraft or Cafe Direct (a trading arm of Oxfam which is now supplied by 214,000 farmers world-wide), have deliberately cultivated a charitable ethos. Community development workers employed by local authorities can often claim to be closer to their beneficieries and publics than some large national charities. Moreover many organisations with social objectives which were once mutual aid networks, voluntary societies or charities, such as the Abbey National, the Co-op movement or the Consumers Association, are now major companies while still retaining some of their ethical goals.

In services there is much the same picture, and charities no longer have a monopoly of care and helping behaviour. The crude myth of the rapacity of for-profit organisations and the essential benevolence of charities in fields such as social care is overstated. Indeed a recent study comparing care provided by private firms with that provided by charities, showed that clients found private care more satisfactory.[14]

The state of the sector

The basic facts

In the UK a long tradition of independent civic action is reflected in high levels of volunteering (51% claimed to have volunteered in 1991, and 31% every month) and in the steady growth of new charities. While older institutions including the traditional churches, trade unions, political parties and some older voluntary organisations (such as the Salvation Army) have experienced declining affiliation, others have grown: particularly organisations involved in green issues (Greenpeace, Friends of the Earth to Earth First), animals (WWF, RSPB and RSPCA), conservation (National Trust to Common Ground), children (SCF, NSPCC), overseas assistance (Oxfam and Action Aid), housing (Shelter to Centrepoint) and health (stretching all the way from Imperial Cancer Research to the Terence Higgins Trust). Many have grown out of user groups (such as Gingerbread) others as arms of government (like Crime Concern).

In addition to 200,000 non-charitable voluntary organisations there are now 170,000 charities, replenished by 4600 newcomers in 1992 and over 12000 in 1993 (temporarily boosted by the new Charities Act).

These vary greatly, including a layer of large, highly
efficient charities which are not greatly different from
medium to large businesses, down to thousands which
are largely dormant. Latest (provisional) estimates suggest
that these together employ 4% of the workforce, 950,000
people, of whom about a third are in education and
research. Total operating income of the sector broadly
defined is estimated at £29.5bn - somewhat more than the
government's education budget, and, if we exclude
recreation, education, the trade unions and business
associations turnover amounts to £12.3bn. For the broadly
defined sector private earned income amounts to £14.2bn
(48%); income from government £11.6bn (39%); and
private giving £3.6bn (12%). For the narrowly defined
sector (which excludes such bodies as sports clubs and
business associations), income includes £5.2bn of private
earned income (42%), £4.3bn of income from government
(35%) and private giving of £2.9bn (23%).[15]

UK Voluntary Sector, 1990
(equivalent to 390,000 full-time employess)

**(This table is based on a narrow definition of the voluntary sector
prepared by Jeremy Kendall and Martin Knapp)**

The economic limits to charitable resources

In economic terms this sector remains marginal. Even in its widest definition it accounts for at most 4% of GDP (rather similar to many other countries which might be expected to have less developed voluntary action). Moreover since the mid-1980s charity revenue has stagnated. While by some criteria government funding has grown, particularly through schemes like the Urban Programme and Single Regeneration Budgets, endemic fiscal pressures have kept spending in check and make it unlikely that there will be much growth in the future.

What is perhaps more surprising is the stagnation of personal giving, even during periods of quite rapid growth in personal disposable income. According to the most recent CAF statistics, an array of incentives such as Gift Aid, tax breaks on covenants and Give as You Earn has failed to raise personal giving, which remains static and predominantly unplanned. Although, according to the Institute of Charitable Fund Managers (ICFM), income for the larger charities has grown rapidly, this seems to have been at the expense of the smaller charities, which lack marketing clout and professionalism.

Some would attribute this stagnation to declining generosity, to confusion or fatigue. There are certainly some signs of all three, although the suggestion that public generosity is declining is hard to square with the huge success of some schemes and the steady growth in revenues of third world charities which one might expect to be the first to suffer from selfish parochialism. Later, we argue that one important factor may simply be the backwardness of many of the forms of charity giving.

But regardless of this, on the horizon there are also other threats to public giving. One is the National Lottery. It is too soon to make a firm judgement on its impact on charitable donations, but international experience suggests that it is unlikely that there will be a net benefit.

Another threat may be the effect of government policies on long-term care for the elderly which may be eating into legacies, which account for much of the voluntary income of many charities: 71% for the Royal National Lifeboat Institution and Cancer Research, 56% for the Salvation Army and 32% for the National Trust.

The charitable impulse in business

Corporate giving, which at one point looked like a significant new source of revenue, remains fixed at a low level. Despite the rhetoric of corporate responsibility, giving remains at barely one-tenth of US levels, at 0.1 - 0.2% of profits compared to 1.8% in the US, although in the UK comparatively more help is given in kind.[16] It is somewhat higher (around 0.5%) for the top 100 companies, but in decline since the late 1980s. If anything the direction of argument may now be back to 'sticking to the knitting', with charity seen as part of overheads, rather than towards greater social responsibility, and the last two years have seen real, and monetary cuts in corporate giving. Milton Friedman's view that business people should not spend 'someone else's money for a general social interest' retains wide support. However, a significant number of businesses are finding that to keep up market positioning an ethical stance is valuable.

As Russell Sparkes' book *The Ethical Investor* shows there is scope for businesses to be responsible: some have found niches by embodying values, like Ben and Jerry's in the USA, Chateau de Lastours in France (which only employs disabled people) and the Body Shop in the UK. Such companies have successfully built up a reputation that enables them to charge an 'ethical premium' for their products. Others, notably Allied Dunbar, have integrated charity into their work, by raising money from their sales force who then determine where it goes.

But the idea of charity as a bolt-on has not proven a success. Instead, as Russell Sparkes put it, 'corporate support for voluntary action in the future is likely to fall into one of two classes: by way of staff motivation and engagement, or as a way of building relationships with customers, with the latter often known as cause-related marketing'.[17]

The conclusion in other words is that charity money, strictly defined, is relatively stagnant. Where there are new sources of ethical money - such as the charity investment funds which may account for as much as £40bn, or the ethical funds which have grown to over £800m - these are not being channelled directly into charitable purposes.

Problems with the heritage

Why should anyone be concerned about mechanisms for encouraging generosity? The heritage of laws and arrangements governing charity has proven remarkably resilient and adaptive. But powerful forces are now calling it into question.

Value shifts
Charity law was established in a predominantly Christian, pre-democratic, and pre-industrial society. In recent years there has been a steady movement away from fixed moral codes, and towards a more personalised morality, more about self-responsibility rather than duty, and as much to do with self-realisation as philanthropy. The attachment to autonomy also makes people less willing to transfer their powers to others. They prefer to do things themselves and there is an almost instinctive hostility to doing things for (as opposed to with) others. Younger people prefer to see beneficiaries speaking for themselves, rather than through an organisation or a celebrity. They also often prefer a more irreverent style of communication, clearer connections between donor and results, more affirmative images replacing those designed to elicit pity, such as with recent posters of the Cerebal

Palsy Society. Finally, a less deferential, more educated public demands tougher standards of integrity and performance from charities just as it does from other organisations such as political parties.

Institutions and governance
Partly because of declining deference governance questions are now central concerns for most major institutions - not just public sector bodies which need to be accountable both directly and indirectly to the general public, but also for the private sector which has been through a long debate about corporate governance. By contrast charities have tended to ignore these concerns, believing that the virtues of their ends justify the means for achieving them. But as they have been drawn into larger roles in service provision and the contract culture, and as fund-raising has become more visible, new questions are arising about governance, codes of conduct, performance measurement, and accountability to beneficiaries. Above all they face the question of representation. Most modern institutions now have clear rules of representation. Company directors represent shareholders. Officeholders represent voters or members. Charities are becoming unusual in that too often they lack any principles of representation, either for members or for beneficiaries and users. Beneficiaries and users have no legal status (although many charities are trying to democratise: one particularly interesting example is Save the Children's attempt to involve children more actively in shaping their policies). This has heightened tensions not only over resources and policies but also, as in the case of some disabilities charities, over the images which are used in the media.

Relations with government
Charities like to think of themselves as independent. But in practice they are substantially dependent, above all on the state; according to the definition used they receive between 35% and 39% of their income from government.

34

This divides between contracts and grants (perhaps surprisingly two-thirds of funding from local government still comes in the form of grants rather than contracts). In the 1980s researchers in the US surprised many by pointing out the extent of dependence on government. In Europe, the state is even more important as a source of funds, traditionally through grant aid or subventions, but increasingly by way of contractual arrangements, at least in France, Austria, and Italy, and even in some east central European states such as Hungary. Even in countries where grants continue to be the main form of state support, government very often accounts for the bulk of the sector's income as in Germany, the Netherlands, and Cataluna, where percentages reach to up to 70%. But dependence on government is also an effect of regulations, which were significantly tightened up in the 1992/3 Charity Acts.

Gender and time
According to Frank Prochaska 'much of the voluntary traditions of modern Britain are deeply rooted in female culture, which found a ...relatively unrestricted avenue for expression in charitable work.' Today by contrast with a majority of women at work, this huge reserve army of volunteers has been disbanded, and those with most time on their hands - the elderly and the unemployed - are the least likely to volunteer. Others have much less free time than in the past, as working hours creep up again and the time taken on activities like driving children to school or shopping mount. According to data collected by Demos, 86% of working women in Britain say they 'never have enough time to get things done' and the average woman now has 14 hours less free time each week than the average man. For charities which used to rest on a base of highly motivated middle-class women this shift in time has been extremely serious.[18]

New needs and desires
Charity law grew up around a particular set of needs,

primarily ones for sustenance. Christian definitions of
charity clarified these with the focus on the poor and
needy. But modern needs are more complex. As societies
develop they tend to move from sustenance-driven needs
(for food or shelter) through outer-directed needs for such
things as status, towards more inner-directed needs for
experience, spiritual and psychological fulfilment. In
modern Britain many still lack basic needs. But for most
of the population an emerging role of charity is to
provide for other needs of self-realisation or exploration.
This is why one of the fastest growth areas in new
charities and non-profit organisations has been around
counselling, self-help and new needs for advice and
information. It is also why new organisations are growing
up around desires, for example for a better quality
environment or a strong local sense of community.

Globalisation
Our frameworks for charity assume fairly impenetrable
national frontiers. Apart from the recent Johns Hopkins
Comparative Non-Profit Sector Project,[19] in most of the
great commissions on the voluntary sector there is almost
no sense of the presence of the outside world, even
though the UK has a particularly strong record in
supporting charity overseas. In the next 10-20 years global
forces are likely to have an increasing impact on the UK.
New European Union programmes are already having an
impact on charitable activity, where in order to receive
funding, partners from different European Union
countries need to be brought in, thus increasing
opportunities for cross-frontier activity. Many UK based
charities operate overseas, not only in poor countries, but
also closer to home: for example Groundwork in Northern
France or Age Concern in Spain, or for that matter CAF in
Russia.

Greater international links are also calling into
question old assumptions and definitions. For example,
France uses the term *economie sociale* to include non-
profits, co-operatives and mutuals, a late 19th century

concept, revived by an alliance of French socialists and Catholic social reformers. In Sweden and Italy too the concept is used to describe the rapidly growing non-profit providers of public services. In Germany, Switzerland and the Netherlands non-profit organisations always maintained their position within frameworks of welfare provision. Internationalisation of both business and the purchase and provision of public services is likely to affect UK charities, not least through the importation of new categories which are incompatible with our traditional definitions and legal framework.

Legal and institutional tension points
The result of these pressures for change is already apparent. Charities sometimes look like anachronisms, their official legal form at odds with their reality. Some squeeze themselves into definitional boxes (such as education) in order to win charitable status. Many have convoluted structures to link them to trading organisations which then covenant all their profits back to the charity (sometimes illegally). Others are set up by highly motivated individuals who have to conjure up trustees to govern them, although they are the instigators and drivers of the organisation.

A series of policy problems is also arising as a direct consequence of charities rising profile. One is unfair competition. Fair competition has come to be widely accepted as a good principle, both in business and in the public sector. There is a growing debate on unfair competition between charities (who get tax breaks) and private sector organisations in the granting and provision of services, which is most developed in the USA and has now reared its head in the UK. There are already rumblings within the Office of Fair Trading and small business complaints are increasing.

There is a similar concern over the tax status of charities, which organisations that provide similar services to charities, for example in social housing or meals for the elderly, feel to be unfair as they represent a subsidy to a particular class of organisation. Tax breaks are targeted at categories of organisation rather than activities that might be deemed to be in the public good or of moral value.

So across many dimensions the heritage of charity law and culture has now run into serious problems, with the heritage increasingly at odds with the most important ethical impulses. In the next section we therefore take the argument a stage further, and examine in detail the primary motivations of voluntary action at the end of the 20th century.

Generosity

Discussions of voluntary and charitable activity usually start with organisation, laws and structures. We focus instead on what drives people to act, and we identify four primary motivations: giving, helping, creating and changing the world.

Giving and receiving
What is generosity? Traditional assumptions about charity have painted it as altruism. In the Bible charity is only legitimate if it is anonymous and not enjoyed. The satisfaction the giver feels is too easily labelled self-satisfaction. But generosity isn't only important for the giver. It is also important for the receiver so that the relationship isn't simply one of passivity and dependence.

Our research suggests that generosity is best understood in terms of relationships and exchange. This is particularly clear in relation to volunteering. Those motivated by the desire to meet people and make friends are more likely to be regular volunteers than those who have other primary motives, such as helping people in need. Commitment to helping activities is closely related to the extent to which people wish to widen and deepen their social networks. Work, leisure, fun and giving thus

become part of a seamless thread. This may be why, in the
Volunteer Centre's surveys on volunteers, the words
'altruism' and 'charity' were found to put people off as
too pure, unattainable or do-gooderish.

Indeed if it was not for this link between generosity
and fun, between charity and self-development, we might
not have such an abundance of generous behaviour.
People voluntarily give 5 billion hours per year - the
equivalent of 600,000 full time jobs.[20] The total voluntary
donations of individuals lie somewhere between £4.8 and
£6.7 billion, approximately 1% of GDP. Importantly it
seems people either give time or money. Trying to turn
donors into volunteers and vice versa may result in either
a fall in donations or a fall in volunteering.[21]

But measures of generosity do not paint a uniform
picture. People on higher incomes, with greater
educational attainments are likely to give and volunteer
more, especially in formal settings,and this activity seems
to peak in middle age. But whilst age and education
remain important indicators of volunteering in
community care there are significant differences. So, for
example, people from lower socio-economic groups are
more likely to be involved in informal voluntary activity,
as are members of black and ethnic minority groups or
women.[22] This evidence supports those who have long
argued that previous surveys of helping activity, by
concentrating exclusively on formal volunteering,
underestimate the contribution of the less well-off.

Part of the reason is that the motivation to help may
require money before it translates into action. Those who
receive out of pocket expenses are more likely to
volunteer on a regular basis, particularly if they are poor.
Similarly, benefits rules discourage the unemployed.

Creating a climate for giving
These statistics show that there is no lack of will for
people to help, give and share. But generosity is not a
particularly rational or consistent motive. Giving remains
remarkably random: the single biggest determinant of

whether people give is whether they are asked, and the biggest determinant of how much they give is their sense of what others are giving.

This randomness remains the biggest problem for those seeking to increase generous behaviour. While other financial arrangements have been modernised with complex new products on offer, charity remains largely stuck in the era of alms and collecting boxes despite the remarkable advances in charity fund-raising and marketing techniques.

But there is also a cultural dimension to generosity - a tone that is set by leading figures in society, and by government itself. For example the appointment of who should run the National Lottery was a major symbolic opportunity to foster generosity. Instead of choosing the consortium led by Virgin and Cable and Wireless, which had promised to donate all profits to charitable activity beyond the already agreed payouts, Camelot was chosen on the grounds of lower costs. Whatever the individual merits of either application, Camelot soon generated substantial profits, running at over £2 million per week, a good proportion of which could have financed the range of proposals we suggest in our conclusions. Yet more important might have been the symbolic pay-offs, which could have been reiterated every week. Instead, Camelot has launched a series of other lotteries, such as Instants, reinforcing the impression that the Lottery is solely about greed and narrow self-interest.

Public generosity and public policy
How does government generosity influence individual generosity? Many believe that state generosity is always by its nature disabling, morally unsustainable, and likely to lead to chronic inefficiencies and bureaucracy. If there is a limited market for generosity, then the state taking more will mean people giving less. The US's greater commitment to charity is sometimes cited in support, and this argument was also commonly used during the 1980s. But it is not easily supported by any historical or

cross-national evidence. Studies in the USA, Canada and the UK have tried to discover whether higher government spending on welfare cuts crowds out donations. But a recent review of the empirical evidence found a consensus that the effect is at most very small, and certainly nowhere near the pound for pound reduction that some on the political New Right had speculated about.[23]

Indeed there may be a small effect in the reverse direction, or 'crowd in'. If government is more generous individuals may be more generous too. This is partly because government expenditure on purchasing services from non-profits may act as a kind of imprimatur of quality to leverage private resources from elsewhere in the economy, partly perhaps because a government signalling of generosity influences private behaviour by encouraging a climate of altruism.

It is certainly hard to find much evidence for the crowding out hypothesis in the UK. The period of rapid growth in public spending coincided with stable giving, and a continuing stream of new organisations such as Oxfam (1943) and War on Want (1952), MIND (1946), The Samaritans (1953), Help the Aged (1963) and the network of nature conservation trusts (1960s) - hardly symptoms of a society that believes its duties to be fulfilled by paying the tax bill. Attempts to model any kind of crowding out, or a fixed pool of altruism that is split between government welfare and private giving, have signally failed.

What conclusions can we draw about generosity? Clearly it is as much about exchange as it about altruism of selflessness. Clearly too it is not a fixed pool, that is shaped directly by what government spends and does. A government that appears mean-spirited may engender a similar response in the communities it governs. Later, we draw on this analysis of generosity as intrinsic to relationships, to describe a range of new measures for harnessing generosity - for linking people's ethical impulses to money.

Mutual help

The second motivation underlying charity is the impulse towards self-help and mutual aid. Sometimes this can be literally 'self-help'. But usually what is involved is better described as mutual help because it takes place in groups.

To understand when and how mutual help works we need to understand its limits; above all the economy of time within which everyone lives. Time is a scarce resource, and in most areas of life we prefer to contract out tasks to others in order to save time. The full exercise of autonomy and control is simply not an option, whether in refuse collection or even organising holidays. In many fields prosperity has brought a steady replacement of self-organised activity with the purchase of goods and services.

We therefore find that mutual help works most strongly in two fields:

● fields where for institutional or cultural reasons people cannot get the support they need and where there is a pressing emotional reason for investing a good deal of time. Health is a good example where professional attitudes combined with institutional inertia meant that people's need for support, counselling and information was not being met.

● areas or groups which are time rich and money poor, usually because of high unemployment or inactive older generations. In these cases people join together to achieve goals because this can be done more effectively or satisfyingly than by any of the available alternatives.

These motives explain the attractions of mutual help. But there is also another dimension. When it works it can encourage a sense of autonomy and power; by empowering it creates ownership, by creating ownership it motivates, increases confidence and effectiveness and a sense of autonomy.

Poverty and mutual help
The main incentives towards mutual help are to be found in areas of high unemployment and economic malaise. Mutual help can fill the gaps in provision of everything from money, to food shops and housing. As commercial institutions like banks and supermarkets have withdrawn from poor areas, mutual help organisations have filled the gap: examples include housing co-ops which number around 900, the 400 credit unions and several hundred local exchange trading schemes (LETS). Other examples include crêches set up on a self-help basis to deal with declining local authority provision and local business schools (as in Ardoyne in Belfast) to encourage local entrepreneurship. Even the rise of car boot sales can be seen as part of the same phenomenon.

The discovery of new needs and mutual help
But self-help also has another important new side: a more political side involving the expression and validation of new needs. Many newer organisations grew out of community development and the women's movement. Both were ideologically committed to enabling individuals and groups to organise themselves, independent of professionals and formal power structures. These include health based self-help groups

such as for specific diseases like cancer, diabetes or Aids; the carers groups; drug addiction advisory organisations; ethnic minority group advisory centres or tenants associations.

This type of organisation provides emotional support, information, advice, practical help, advocacy and campaigning. They are in part a revolt against government and professionals (although many work in tandem with professionals), building up their own base of knowledge - and also putting pressure on the state. Many are ephemeral in nature - set up to deal with a specific issue that may go away, or vulnerable to the departure of a key individual. Others become national organisations like the Breast Care and Mastectomy Association or umbrella bodies like Cancerlink.

Beyond professionalism
All of these different types of organisation share some features, above all a rejection of the dominant approaches to defining and resolving problems of the professions. For the professional approach to problem-solving favours structures that are formal rather than informal, decision making that is hierarchical rather than participative, language that is often jargonistic rather than everyday. Moreover the professional public bodies tend to provide services rather than support or information, are paid for rather than relying on voluntary labour, and base their knowledge on science and training rather than direct experience.

Mutual help organisations by contrast value experience, flat structures and participation. In this respect their central principles are little different from their equivalents a century or more ago. As Stan and Mari Thekaekara, who founded ACCORD, an Indian integrated community development organisation working with the tribes people of Gudalur, aptly put it on a visit to the UK:

'Communities have to understand that it is their problem, not that they have created it, but that they are the only people who can find true solutions to it.

Undoubtedly they will need help and support, both
financially and in terms of human resources, this is
where NGOs or professionals come in. But when people
speak of participation it often only means participation in
terms of labour and local materials, occasionally in
decision making, but very rarely community control over
the whole process where the NGO or specialist becomes
only a catalyst that sooner or later will outlive their
usefulness. If a community can take control over all
aspects of their lives we will see true change.'[24]

This is very distinct from charity. As one resident in
Easterhouse (visited by Thekaekara) put it: 'We are used to
poverty, but we can't handle charity'. Much the same
perspective encouraged the growth of the mutual aid
movement in the 19th century which tried to deal with
needs by creating friendly societies of every kind from
coffin clubs, to penny banks, penny schools and penny
doctors, to avoid relying on the hand-outs of the poor law.
Even then this was contrasted with receiving charity.
Colin Ward suggests similarities between modern urban
Britain and the situation of rural Britain at the beginning
of the 19th century. Like then a significant proportion of
the population has little income generating capacity and
has to find new forms of business based more on co-
operation.

Barriers and support structures
Many self-help bodies can in practice gain charitable
status, even though they technically fall foul of the
prohibition of gain. But they still face serious barriers.
One is that the cost of running charities is rising, another
is that the obligations are cumbersome. The various jobs
of accounting to the Charity Commission, adhering to the
SORP accountancy requirements and the Charities Act,
evaluating outputs and outcomes, getting trustees and
committee members trained for the job, and dealing with
tax reclaims, all add up to an expensive burden. Self-help
activities generally require simpler structures, trust,
small amounts of money that are granted with few

questions asked.

As they grow many self-help organisations find they need some support. Several different models exist and have been proposed for providing a supportive structure, and for making it easier for communities to borrow and use capital. The Rowntree Foundation sponsored report 'Investing in People', focused on Community Development Trusts as an effective model for harnessing local resources. These have now taken a wide range of forms. Examples include traditional housing associations like the Notting Hill Housing Trust, which has put over £750,000 into community type developments not concerned with housing; traditional settlements like Toynbee Hall, and the Blackfriars and Birmingham Settlements which are retooling to meet today's needs; trusts such as Coin St. Developers, North Kensington Amenity Trust, or the Inner City Trust in Derry which grew out of crisis, campaigning or oppositional politics; and sponsored trusts like Moss Side and Hulme or Govan which have developed out of TECs or the local authority.

What they all share is a capital base or endowment, which generates rents and other money to make investments that traditional financing would shy away from. This resource represents the docking point for other initiatives to start such as food co-ops or credit unions, and through their links they can capitalise on other programmes. The Flax Trust in Ardoyne in Belfast is a good example. They bought two old linen mills and transformed one and a half into enterprise workshops. From that base they set up a business school for local training, a housing co-op, a community programme, an elderly persons complex, several local shops, as well as a number of companies. In total 80 firms operate within the trust's orbit, employing 900 people. Some of these through family connections have special links to the US, where they have become sub contractors or franchisees of small American companies wanting to get into Europe. They import social entrepreneurs and develop them locally. And, most importantly in the Belfast context, firms and employees are equally split between Protestants and Catholics.

These trusts provide shelter, a certain culture and confidence for those that want to start projects. They do not own all the initiatives themselves, which are instead usually spun off and take on a life of their own. They have parallels to the incubator units found in science parks.

Limits of mutual help

Some like to romanticise mutual help and suggest it as a generalisable model for restructuring the whole of society and the economy away from dependence on large corporate or government systems. Writers ranging from Ivan Illich to Murray Bookchin have made this argument. There are indeed substantial opportunities to create new forms of mutual organisation - club type structures within which people can exchange time for goods for example, or self-build housing organisations, or shared systems for providing education. But such accounts fall down on several crucial counts.

● They ignore the issue of time. With a scarcity of time we can only invest participative energy in a small number of outlets. It is usually far more efficient to delegate a job to others. The exceptions come only when something is of very close personal concern - such as an illness - or where time is sufficiently abundant.

● They ignore the wider economic questions of power and money. Mutual help without some resources is often futile, giving only the semblance of control. This is why there is often a logical development from mutual help into political engagement as it becomes clear that a problem - such as Aids or jobs - cannot be solved without external support.

● Many mutual help groups are ephemeral and fleeting. Indeed their ease of creation and the ease with which they disappear is one of their strengths. To expect them to become a permanent organising principle is unrealistic.

● When this is not the case they tend to become professionalised and more distant from their origins. This was certainly true of many 19th and early 20th century mutual help organisations in Britain and Germany which evolved into hierarchical, bureaucratic organisations. In itself this is not necessarily bad; but it suggests the need to be realistic about the life-cycles of organisations which rarely remain fixed in one form.

Helping mutual help
How then should mutual help be supported? The best way is simply to make it easy to operate, with minimal regulations and accounting requirements under a certain level of turnover (see law section for further details). With a supportive regulatory framework there is a case for some modest support structures - either in the form of Community Trusts or in the form of specific initiatives for mutual help such as the Nottingham Self-Help team.[25] These can be funded relatively cheaply.

These are some obvious starting points. But imaginative governments and local authorities might also seek to encourage more radical approaches. For example, programmes could be more deliberately tailored to the nature of time rich, money poor communities. One option for example would be for government to offer grant aid for capital in exchange for local commitments to input time. For example a community group might commit to putting in 500 hours over next 6 months in exchange for a commitment to £1,000 of public money. The CONNECT scheme proposed by Demos as an umbrella for mutual aid and community service is another example,[26] which makes a link between the self-interest of the unemployed and the wider community interest. Other options might involve clubs providing meals for the unemployed in exchange for a certain number of days work each year.

Creativity and social innovation

A third motive is the motive to create - to identify new
needs, explore new solutions and assist in the process of
societal change and invention. This role has been
undervalued. Some forget that not all inventions are
technological. The 19th century invented not only
technologies like the telephone and electricity but also
such things as state pensions and probation. The 20th
century invented both the computer and the radio phone-
in. We know a lot about the sources of technical
innovations, and a panoply of institutions and tax
incentives exists to support it. But much less thinking has
been done about social invention and how it can be
supported, although we know that, like technologies,
successful social innovations tend to be replicated widely,
they become like Richard Dawkins' 'memes', the social
equivalent of genes, mutating and evolving even as they
spread.

Historically the voluntary sector has played a decisive
role in identifying new social needs and devising new
social solutions. Many of the roles of the modern public
sector in schools, hospitals, welfare and penal policy were
pioneered by charities (and for a long time it was assumed
that there was a steady transition from the voluntary

sector into public provision). The voluntary sector acted as a testbed, ironing out the flaws and misconceptions before a new invention spread either into government or into the market. They also acted, and still do act, as a form of market research: identifying and responding to new needs ahead of the market and formal politics. This was as true of Barnardos or the Salvation Army in the 19th century as it is of the Natural Death Centre or the Prison Ashram Trust today.

Much of the fertility of modern life comes from the margins, and thrives in the grey areas between the state, the market and voluntary action. As Vaclav Havel argued in *The Power of the Powerless*, power often stifles creativity and ideas, and only those on the margins have the space, sometimes the eccentricity, to think radically. However, once established such inventions can become successful parts of the mainstream. Examples include The Open University as well as the University of the Third Age, the Consumers Association, Neighbourhood Watch schemes, Guardian Angels, Live Aid and Comic Relief, Chad Varah's Samaritans and local LETS schemes. The Big Issue and Médecins Sans Frontières are others. There is even an organisation - The Institute of Social Inventions - that champions their cause.

In some respects social inventions parallel innovation in business. Like business innovations it is essential that any new form soon finds an economic base - groups of users or members giving money, state contracts, or people who are prepared to give time instead of money. There are also some parallels in terms of the importance of the overall environment and culture: the rapidity of feedback from user groups; vertical integration of innovation (so that inventions do not simply pop up unformed from the brains of inventors); and a culture that encourages lateral connections and ideas. But in other respects non-profit organisations are very different: because there is no traditional return on investment they are always harder to get off the ground, and few get public funding in their early days because they rarely fit into existing governmental definitions or budget headings. Moreover they are often removed from existing networks of power and influence that govern public funding.

Every age its inventiveness
Every age needs some social inventiveness. But there are grounds for believing that the scope for social innovation is particularly large at the moment when many existing institutions are showing signs of strain and when many social problems such as social cohesion, jobs creation, inner-city decay and youth unemployment seem resistant to orthodox solutions.

Even a cursory visit to any urban part of Britain shows how much the voluntary sector is in the forefront of devising new solutions. Initiatives are sprouting everywhere, sometimes unfunded but often around the edge of the public sector, in education or community care, environmental improvement or the assertion of an ethnic identity. This isn't to say that charities are always innovative: many older charities remain profoundly resistant to change and a recent Rowntree study on innovation in the voluntary sector found that, contrary to conventional wisdom, the most innovative were often those most dependent on government contracts, which provide the resources to take innovative risks.

Unfortunately, we cannot simply assume that necessity will always call forth invention. To work, most ideas need to be developed and debugged, without the benefit of laboratories to do this in. Most need money, time and commitment. In this chapter we have therefore set out some of the conditions for encouraging more creativity and social invention.

Creating an environment conducive to innovation
Social entrepreneurs
The first requirement is people. Today we would describe them as social entrepreneurs, people displaying capacities of leadership, inspiration and the capacity to get things done but within communities, either geographical ones

or communities of interest.

Their motivations and skills vary widely. These are a few examples. Chris Elphick instigated the painting of Easterhouse's giant community mural a decade ago, which started the renewal of that community's self-confidence. This required motivational, organisational, and management skills as well as imagination. Jackie Loftus who chairs Clapton Park Estates Comprehensive Estates Initiative, an organisation that has institutionalised and extended tenant power aimed at regenerating five of Hackney's more ravaged estates. As the owner of a local dog grooming parlour she describes herself as a 'born organiser'. Betty Westwood was one of the founders of the Breast Care and Masectomy Association. She was diagnosed with breast cancer in 1968, started researching the cancer education field and found that nothing much was being done to educate the public. Barbara Croft started a group 'Drinking to Cope' for women with drinking problems in rural Derbyshire and established a network for meetings as most members were afraid to meet in their local villages because of gossip. Bob Salisbury took over the Garibaldi School in Clipstone, Nottinghamshire and transformed one of the worst schools in the county to one of the better. He realised early on that to turn around the school he needed more money than government would be able to provide and raised it through a range of innovative partnerships.

These are just a few of the current unsung heroes. There have been many others in the past, notably Michael Young founder of dozens of organisations including the Consumer Association, Henri Poincare founder of the Red Cross or Alec Dickson who founded Voluntary Services Overseas and Community Voluntary Services in the UK.

What these people share is a combination of social commitment and entrepreneurship. Entrepreneurship is normally only associated with business life - seeking and identifying opportunities that are brought to market through products and services. But the essential features of entrepreneurship can exist in any context, and they can be learnt.

Money
At crucial stages almost any social innovation or new institution requires funding to put it into practice. This may be a short-term or one-off grant from a foundation. It may be a contract or series of contracts from government. And it may come from tapping a user base that is prepared and able to pay for a service. The failure to raise any funding usually means that an invention is still-born, however good it may be in other respects.

But money isn't always the solution. It is striking how often lack of money has been a spur to creativity around the voluntary sector, as people learn how to mobilise resources - buildings, skills and so on - without money. In these initial phases too much money, and too much dependence on an external source, can actually inhibit innovation.

Catalyst pressures
Innovations rarely happen in isolation. Energies will only be sparked off if a crisis, challenge or opportunity is recognised. Not all crises are constructive. Some are so endemic and deep-seated that they threaten to overwhelm communities. The catalytic pressures needed to encourage social innovations can take many forms, such as a collapse of public provision, or old job sources. They may arise too from positive opportunities, like the arrival of an outsider. This has been the case with Pat Conaty - an American currently working in Birmingham Settlement who is developing a community bank, using his experience from the USA. The same was true of Ed Berman, an American who set up Interaction - a trust that developed a range of innovative approaches to social renewal such as creating city farms or developing community arts programmes with unemployed youth.

A responsive government
Governments - national and local - can choose to be
understanding and supportive, avoiding unnecessary
rules and restrictions. They can be supportive and
responsive, and in the right circumstances can
deliberately devolve power downwards to encourage
people to put in the time and energy to make innovations
work. If power is jealously guarded energetic people will
sensibly direct it elsewhere. For the same reasons many of
the most innovative solutions in dealing with social
problems have sought to assert self-reliance and
independence.

A culture that accepts the new
Innovative projects are generally driven by committed
even obsessed, original and sometimes eccentric
individuals and their 'creative and innovative deviance'.
To foster social invention it's important that this is
positively sanctioned and that there is a climate at ease
with new ideas, taking risks and making experiments.

Weak barriers
Finally social innovations often depend on the potential
barriers being relatively weak. There is no shortage of
such barriers: for example professional groups that use
entry restrictions, accreditation and the like to block new
ideas. In the case of alternative medicine, for example, the
judges of its effectiveness were usually the very doctors
whose practices were being questioned. Similarly if a new
educational method, such as programmed learning, is
likely to dispense with teachers it is hardly surprising that
they will block it. Equally research and innovation in
prisons that is assigned to prison officials will inevitably
block out certain options. There is also often a culture
clash with government. Accountability to electorates
tends to slow down the pace of response to problems. The
need for reliable services puts a premium on certainty
rather than risk, professional power rather than
voluntary action, balancing of competing interests rather

55

than expression of a particular vision.

The need for pilot projects
How then should we think about this social R&D function
and the role of creative voluntary action? And how could
public policy do more to deliberately encourage it?

Although some industries have well developed
research and development the public sector has little,
except in medicine. Policies tend to be tried out at a
national level rather than properly market tested and
appraised - the National Curriculum and the Poll Tax are
obvious examples. The justification usually given is that
the public expects uniform and standardised solutions
and does not take kindly to differentiated policies. There
are some pressures away from this rather odd
conventional wisdom, with the encouragement of pilot
projects. Often these are easier to organise at one remove
from government in the voluntary sector, since there are
less pressures for standard career structures, job security
and conventional control mechanisms. Once tested a
project can then be rolled out within the public sector.
The problem at present, however, is that there are no
specific R&D budgets within the public sector and no
formalised means of policy appraisal. Moreover existing
fiscal incentives for R&D, which provide 100% write-off
against profits, are of no use to non-profit organisations.

Hothousing innovation
There is a range of mechanisms which can be deliberately
encouraged to speed up the process. Some are technical
and mechanistic, while others entail a shift in culture.

● A deliberate use of resources to support innovation
with a percentage of public spending directed to
voluntary organisations - perhaps 0.5% initially - to be
deliberately directed to social risk initiatives.
● Legal reform could make it easier for social
entrepreneurs to sit as executive trustees etc., ending the
pretence that trustees are the legal 'owners' of an initiative.

● A cultivation of open networks and responsive styles of government, and further direction of funding towards collaborative projects which make links across sectoral boundaries, would help.

● A better organisation of appraisal, to identify good innovations early and encourage their emulation, in an equivalent to technology transfer.

There also some more lateral ways of encouraging innovation. Celebratory events, such as local festivals, can bring people together around a sense of common purpose (one example was the project Glasgow Lit Up involving 10,000 people in making lanterns and lights. This subsequently effected the lighting policy of the city, which in turn reduced crime and improved perceptions of safety in the city). The Drumlarnock Road project, also in Glasgow, involved two youth gangs who were constantly at loggerheads, in a play that over three months brought them together, showing not only the social impact of the arts, but also providing the social services department with lessons about dealing the social tension.

Competitions, prizes and public acclamations are another way of achieving this objective. They are currently limited to architectural, urban design, garden festival and arts projects, but could also be used for social experiments, such how to deal with drugs and crime, for developing environmental friendly solutions to estate management or economic development initiatives that successfully create jobs for young people.

The generation of the tender documents themselves would provide opportunities to mixed groups of people, from the public, private and voluntary organisations, to gather together to create portfolios of ideas and solutions to social problems. These open processes can be instrumental in looking at problems and opportunities afresh.

But the most important factor may simply be a cultural one: an acknowledgement of the R&D role of the voluntary sector.

Making change - politics and charity

Power and influence
Our fourth area is politics: the connection of ethical
dispositions to the larger needs of the society or even the
planet. This view of things would have been almost
wholly alien to the drafters of the original charity
legislation. For in the 16th century charity was a personal
and religious affair. Few expected the state to solve social
problems. Instead politics was primarily about statecraft,
above all defending the borders from attack.

But in a democratic era perceptions are very different.
People's moral instincts spill over into politics, which is
never confined to the pursuit of self-interest. They
automatically go beyond the face to face help of charity.
And they fit in with a universal disposition to become
part of larger purposes - a role once played predominantly
by religion. Today for example, according to MORI
Socioconsult, 38% of 18-20 year olds say that their ideal
career would be 'one where I could become both
politically and socially involved', and 74% say that 'we are
all responsible for what goes on in the world', and 64% of
15-17 year olds say that 'mankind deserves to die out if we
do not start caring properly for the environment'. Not all
of these sentiments are reflected in action. But they do

reflect a culture in which politics in its widest sense has become mainstream, even though few have much enthusiasm for politics in its formal senses.

The motivations for engagement of this kind are complex. But we often underestimate the fulfilment people get. Albert Hirschman quotes Golda Meir on why she came to Israel in the 1920s: 'When I heard what was being done here I decided that they're not going to do it by themselves. I won't have a share in it? No I must be a part of it. Just pure selfishness I suppose...'[27] More generally there is a pleasure from the goals, the camaraderie, the striving to achieve change, that can be reduced neither to the explanations from interests, nor simply to a commitment to ethical principles. Perhaps this was why John Stuart Mill thought participation in public affairs would 'guard against passivity, inertia, timidity and intellectual stagnation...'

This type of motivation - an identification with a larger interest - has been central to voluntary action for at least two centuries. But changemaking, as opposed to amelioration, has never sat easily within the tradition of charity law and these tensions have tended to increase rather than decrease, because as democracy has filtered deep into our culture the lines between charity and change have become steadily less clear.

When people become involved in charity they find it hard to remain satisfied either with paternalistic giving or self-help. Whether the field is housing or Aids, animal welfare or education, it is hard not to engage with the larger, politically influenced systems of provision. As a result, around modern politics there is now a broad range of pressure points - campaigns like Friends of the Earth or the National Viewers and Listeners Association, making arguments, devising policies, complaining and arguing, but also sharing some of the attributes of traditional charity. Only rarely do these have a simple and focused role. Instead many combine service delivery with public argument, accountability to a membership with bidding for contracts (and few are visibly stifled in their campaigning by contracts).[28]

Although some are financially dependent on
government, many of these organisations form part of the
informal opposition to those in power. After all, insiders
rarely need to organise visibly and formally, but can
instead use discrete channels of influence. Most have
historically been allied to the left or centre of politics,
although many of the most effective single issue groups
of recent years have come from the right, campaigning,
for example, against abortion or pornography in
broadcasting. Taken as a whole such organisations now
have much larger memberships than the political parties
and can often claim an authority that politicians lack.

Some view this politicisation as malign. On the left the
fear is that this weakens the role of the political party in
representing broad interests; that it tends to reflect
middle-class interests; and weakens the capacity of
government to take strategic decisions.

The case against campaigns
But it is the right-wing argument against the rise of
pressure politics which has in recent years been more
influential: above all their argument that it tends to
overload the state with demands for regulations, spending
programmes and protection. This view was most
coherently developed through the 1970s and 1980s by the
'public choice' school of economists, by the later work of
the economist and philosopher, Friedrich Hayek in his
trilogy, *Law, Legislation and Liberty*[29] and by the economist,
Mancur Olson, particularly in his book, *The Rise and Fall of
Nations*.[30]

Their argument raises major issues for the notion that
politics is a dimension that arises from helping behaviour
and the moral senses. For far from seeing them as benign
expressions, this group of writers argues that the overall
mix of groups of this kind is bound to be
unrepresentative, organising small rather than large
groups. Moreover citizens always seek more from the state
than they are willing to pay for, encouraging politicians

to over-promise, forcing up taxes, fuelling inflation and tending to raise debts for future generations. Worse, the growth of interest groups tends to reduce the scope for political manoeuvre, and politicians try to balance powerful interests, encouraging gridlock and government failure. In the end they warn, economic growth slows down, and everyone is worse off.

To save us from this fate Hayek made the case for restrictions on liberty, arguing that 'the new powers created by the perfection of organisational techniques, and by the right conceded to them by existing laws, will probably require limitations by general rules of law far more narrow than those it has been found necessary to impose by law on the actions of individuals.'[31] This view has many supporters, though they rarely feel comfortable making them publicly: more often the case is made tangentially, for example through arguments for using constitutional reform to remove key issues, such as monetary policy or free trade, from political debate.

The case for pluralism
Against this stands an opposite view. This is the argument that the rise of campaigns and arguments is precisely a virtue of democratic societies, making it more likely that society will innovate, evolve and discover truth. It is a case made forcibly by Perri 6, who quotes John Stuart Mill's comment that 'truth, in the great practical concerns of life, is so much a question of the reconciling and combining of opposites, that ... it has to be made in the rough process of a struggle between combatants fighting under hostile banners.'[32] From this stems the belief that free competition in ideas is in the general interest, and that we should therefore encourage the maximum pluralism in political organisation, campaigning and argument.

James Madison gave this argument one of its clearest expressions in the Federalist Papers when he argued that freedom of speech not only provides a framework that encourages campaigns to be honest, and through their conflicts to arrive at truth: it also encourages a culture of responsibility and respect.[33] A key point is that no one can know in advance which potential speaker will make the most important contribution to the debate; it is therefore sensible to allow everyone their say, subject to the ground rules of that debate, as part of a societal discovery process.

Perri 6 argues that, 'as the campaigns of pressure groups and lobbies compete with each other, they begin to act like firms in a market, where policy-makers and the public are the consumers of that information. Most importantly, they compete in producing information with which they seek to criticise, refute, and undermine information offered by their rivals....Campaigning groups and organisations invest in their reputation for expertise and trustworthiness: this is one market force for better quality policy information. It does the effectiveness of a pressure group no good to have a reputation among policy-makers for providing unreliable information. Although the market does not produce perfect or complete information, it provides some incentives for anyone with relevant information to offer it on the market place, for fear it will be ignored and its relevance for policy go unappreciated, or that the person or group offering it, will be sidelined.'[34]

Our guess is that this view of the virtues of a free market for ideas is widely shared. Certainly those advocating restrictions run almost immediately into doubts about their true motives.

But another reason is simply that the argument for pluralism fits with history. The rise of associations and single issue campaigns reflects the inability of the traditional political parties - most with their roots in the 19th or early 20th century - to adequately reflect the multiplicity of views and interests. Symptoms of this include the relative memberships of parties and campaigns. In the UK today, for example, the major parties both have well under 500,000 members, considerably less than environmental, animal or conservation organisations.

The wider argument is that the rise of associations reflects a shift in the focus of politics away from interests and class towards broader life issues - ethics, meaning, purpose. Thus politics comes to be organised as much around issues such as abortion or roads, the conservation of town centres or animal rights, as around the classic model of a battle around economic interests. Any examination of the leading voluntary organisations of the day confirms this shift in focus. While trade unions, mainstream churches and many 19th century charities are continuing their long decline, campaigns around the ecology, animal rights, sexual politics, roads and so on are in the ascendant.

The problem in the UK, however, is that the legal frameworks of political action have not evolved to reflect this reality. The law actually inhibits a full expression of this connection between individual concerns and public debate. Indeed charities are today the only institutions without full rights of free speech because of the prohibition against their full engagement in politics.

The justifications for this focus on the tax advantages of charities: it is argued that governments should not support controversy or provide charities with an advantage over for profits. Moreover, donors who in fact want to support services, should be protected from unwittingly supporting political goals.

This may sound like a rather arcane dispute. But in fact these issues have at times gained a very high profile, with sharp criticisms by regulators of charities like Oxfam and War and Want for exceeding the bounds of charity and seeking to influence government policy, for example on aid. But as a *Times* leader pointed out (17th May 1991) if donors are unhappy with an organisation's political activities it is surely better for them to cease giving than for the state to intervene. As they put it 'in the end, the market itself will regulate charitable involvement in politics'.

The rise of associations

But the best reason for doubting the continued relevance of this old prohibition is that the clear line between politics and other areas of life has been made obsolete by the growing commitment to participation. Contrary to a popular view that modernity has wiped out civil society, as we have already seen, most available evidence suggests that it is as strong as ever. Indeed the rise of associations is one of the distinctive features of the modern world. In parallel with the rise of complex systems of provision in economics and science people's willingness to form associations to achieve change has steadily risen.

According to a 1982 study by Lester Salamon 65% of the organisations in 16 US communities had been created since 1960. Each of the major social movements of the last 40 years - the civil rights movement, feminism, environmentalism, conservative moralism - has roots in the voluntary sector. In France associations are being formed at five times the rate of the 1960s, and in the UK charity registration is taking place at a far faster rate than in the 1960s.[35]

Western societies - and many less developed nations - seem to be becoming more like the vision of America that de Tocqueville expressed in his famous *Democracy in America* - based on dense networks of civic associations. He famously argued that 'among the laws that rule human societies there is one which seems to be more precise and clear than all others. If men are to remain civilised or to become so, the art of associating together must grow and improve in the same ratio in which equality of condition is increased.'

In part this shift towards associations reflects changing perceptions of the state in the wake of the crisis of socialism. After the 1940s it seemed legitimate to focus politics around demands on the state, right across the world. But the disillusion with state provision has led to a marked shift in the nature of the politics-charity relationship, a rethinking of faith in administration and professionals and a revisiting of older traditions of self-reliance and mutual help. Considering less developed countries one study wrote 'antipoverty programs that the official political-administrative hierarchy designs and implements in a heavily, almost exclusively top-down fashion tend to be ineffective ...,'[36] a World Bank Official said 'we overestimated what governments could do.'[37]

In a sense this is returning us to a 19th century view of change as no longer monopolised by the formal structures of party politics and government. Instead the desire to achieve social change works through multiple avenues - self-help, personal responsibility, local action, as well as demands for funded programmes or legislation.

In part it reflects the collapse of arguably the most important political movement of this century, the communists. Since there is now no movement promising total systemic change, every organisation has to engage with the power structure as it is, dealing in a much more complex mix of argument and co-option, and the redefinition of external demands by powerholders themselves.

Nor does this desire to achieve change respect national boundaries. There are an estimated 4,600 Western voluntary organisations active in the developing world, supporting another 20,000 indigenous non-profit organisations, which take little heed of the contrast between charity and politics, or for that matter politics and religion. And there is a growing range of genuinely transnational non-profit organisations, ranging from Amnesty International to Médecins Sans Frontières.

In each case the rise of associations has thrown up new points of pressure. In the western world it is the relation with party politics that is most fraught - the subject of continuing debate in the UK with the Charity Commission. In other countries the concern is not that charities are putting undue pressure on the state, but rather that the state is purchasing the support of the voluntary sector. Lester Salamon for example cites the cases of the Harambee in Kenya, and non-profits in Thailand where government has overtly used funding as a political tool. Within the UK too many fear that over-dependence on government contracts necessarily reduces charities independence - their capacity to represent groups in need.

There are legitimate concerns here. Certainly the case for strict rules on elections remains strong. US experience in trying - and largely failing - to restrain an excess of money around politics serves as a warning to other countries. Those seeking elected office should certainly be restrained in what they can do and who they can be funded by. But beyond these a mature democracy should be able to sustain a much looser ecology of argument, and to respect the natural links between service provision and political activity. Indeed in a fully developed society it should be natural to see politics not in narrow terms of party advantage and office-seeking: but rather as part of a spectrum of ways in which people expand their sense of self-interest and find wider goals in which to immerse themselves.

A modernised framework for law and tax

We have described some of the core themes which underlie the other invisible hand: basic values and principles that most people express in everyday action and language. What then are the tools for giving them expression, for nurturing them? In this section we describe some of the tools and policies: legal frameworks, the definition of public goods and new uses of indicators.

Laws: choice in organisational form

The starting point is law. Anyone becoming a trustee or forming a new charity is likely to be astonished to read the necessary legal documents. These are usually written in obscure and archaic English, may restrict the activities the organisation would eventually want to undertake, and are almost invariably hard to understand. But does the law relating to organisations need to be so complex and restrictive? Essentially, there are three functions that law carries out in this area.

First, *legal structures* define the range of forms that organisations can choose. Broadly, English law recognises unincorporated associations (which have no legal personality independently of their individual members), trusts (in the simplest cases, also without legal personality), friendly societies, industrial and provident societies, co-operatives, companies limited by guarantee, and companies limited by share capital.

Second, the law of *legal status* defines the extent to which the courts can enforce certain financial obligations against particular stakeholders. The crucial test here is whether or not an organisation is charitable. If it is, then the monies it lawfully receives must be applied for the purposes specified in its charitable objects and for no other purposes.

Finally, the law of *tax status* defines the fiscal liability of the organisation on its income, expenditures and assets. We postpone discussion of tax matters until a later section.

Take legal structure first. The job that the law of legal structure performs is to provide a basic definition of the extent to which individual stakeholders have 'property rights' in the organisation, that is, the extent to which they have 'ownership' claims on any surplus it may make over and above its costs, as well as their associated responsibilities and rights in the organisation. Clearly, the greater the 'ownership' rights that a stakeholder possesses, the greater the risk they are exposed to, and the greater the rewards they may gain from the success of the organisation as well as the greater their claim to be involved in governance and decision-taking. In general, the law tries to follow this principle.

Given the vast multiplicity of different types of voluntary organisation the range of legal organizational possibilities for bodies with public good objectives is surprisingly narrow, for example:

● In a company limited by shares, the shareholders are full owners. They have every incentive to use their decision-making power to ensure that the organisation is efficient, because the greater the surplus achieved over costs, the greater will be their rewards - in the value of their shares and in the size of their dividend cheques. In a limited company, their risk is limited to the value of their shares.

- The company limited by guarantee, by contrast, creates somewhat fewer incentives for efficiency. In the type most commonly used by non-profit companies, 'shareholders' contribute no capital and their liability for loss is limited to the sum of £1 (unless they have been trading when insolvent). Therefore they are not putting their personal assets at risk. In non-profit companies of this sort, they have no claim on any surplus, and few incentives to act to ensure efficiency. The same is largely true for industrial and provident societies as well as friendly societies, each of which has a base membership.

- The unincorporated association on the other hand, of which there are over 100,000, offers participants no limitation on risk. Unincorporated associations have no legal personality and committee members are personally liable for any debts.

- The trust structure is very similar. There is much fine detail, such as the need - in charitable trusts - for at least three outside trustees who have a duty of care to the beneficiaries, but are prohibited from taking any benefit personally from the organisation, and therefore have no very strong financial incentive for efficiency, other than the long stop threat of legal action in a breach of trust case. In fact, however, trustees liability has been left unlimited in the new Charities Act. Indeed it has been argued that if more charitable trustees were fully aware of this there might be mass resignations.

Next, consider the effect of the law of legal status. Non-profit companies limited by guarantee, friendly and industrial and provident societies, trusts and unincorporated associations may all be charitable, but companies limited by shares may not. Moreover, charitable status is still based on the trust concept. In effect, whatever the structure of a body with charitable objectives, a kind of trust is implied into it by the law. Since the liability of directors of a company limited by guarantee is limited, while that of trustees is not, there is a problem for charitable companies. The usual lawyer's advice is that an individual board member's liability is limited as a director but not as a trustee! In effect, one of the major advantages - protection from risk of failure - is removed, but one of the most important incentives for efficiency - opportunity personally to gain from success - is not provided in compensation. This is surely poor public policy.

More generally, it is far from obvious that this range of legal structures, or the restriction of charitable status to this sub-set, is the ideal design given the proliferation of organisations.

While charities engaged in relatively minor activities, the law of legal structure was rarely a problem. But with their rise in prominence, their growing role in the economy, and more acute battles over governance, we need a broader debate about the law of organisations.

As the non-profit world is becoming more commercial in many ways, the division between a non-commercial structure with unlimited risk but no efficiency incentive and a commercial one with the reverse basis, is no longer useful or appropriate.

We want organisations to be efficient, wherever possible, but we don't want to place everyone who might want to set up or be involved in running an organisation under legal exposure to risk so extensive that they would be deterred from taking part. The time has come to question whether the constraint against the distribution of financial rewards for successful performance, in the world of community-based and mission-driven organisations, is particularly useful, and where it is useful, whether it should be combined with unlimited liability.

There are other difficulties. Many people want to set up mission-driven organisations, but don't want to deal with boards of trustees. They would rather run their own show. This is very common in such fields as residential care for the elderly. They must therefore choose to set up an ordinary company, which may not be their first choice.

Why should a choice to be non-profit also be a choice to be saddled with a management structure that the entrepreneur who creates the organisation doesn't find helpful? There is no compelling public policy reason why organisations should be required to have a board if they are non-profit. However, there might be a case for saying that someone who wants complete protection from risk to their personal capital ought, in certain kinds of organisations, to be expected to contribute some capital. At the moment, the bare non-charitable company limited by guarantee asks remarkably little of its board of directors, and has few incentives for efficiency.

Should we, then, try to design a new single system of legal structure and legal status for all organisations? There is no great merit in the idea that all organisations should have the same structure. People ought to be able to set up their organisation with whatever structure they please, subject to certain public policy constraints. What is needed is legislation that defines a set of building blocks from which each project can design the organizational form appropriate to their needs. The choices to be made would include:

● Whether to distribute any part of any surplus over production costs to organisation members, or to board members in the form of dividends, increases in invested asset values or by honoraria.

● Whether to have a membership with governing rights.

● How clearly to define core purposes, and how these can be changed.

● Whether beneficiaries or users should have formal legal claims upon the organisation for services.

● Whether to have a board of non-executive persons responsible for governance.

● Whether to set limits on personal rewards for employees (since very large rewards can, presumably, undermine the meaningfulness of the non-distribution constraint, if there is one).

71

- Capital/risk ratios that might be allowable in particular circumstances.

These are decisions to be made by those creating organisations. External accountability for all kinds of organisation should lie primarily through accounting requirements and the stipulations attached to public funds. Beyond these there should be wide freedom to develop appropriate organisational forms.

It is important not to over-estimate the importance of structures of ownership and governance. In the debate about corporate governance of large firms since the Cadbury Report and the RSA report on *Tomorrow's Company*, there has been a tendency to assume that getting governance right is the central public policy concern about organisations. One can make out a good argument that part of the problem of the law of organisations is that we have, for almost a century and a half, spent too much time and energy trying to get it 'right', when there are no universally right answers.

The categories of joint-stock company, charitable trust, friendly or industrial and provident society and unincorporated association were only fixed and defined in their modern form in the nineteenth century. That was one of the great periods of innovation and diversification in the forms of organisations. We are now living through another such period. Community businesses, new local partnerships and hybrid bodies, board-remunerating non-profit bodies, and bodies that don't want to have to choose between many of the forms on offer can now be found in any major British city. At a time when new types of organisation are emerging that just don't naturally fit the existing categories, we should stop trying to design law that will suit them, and let them suit themselves.

In conditions of free choice of organisational form, it would be for those providing gifts, donations, grants, service agreements and contracts to determine how organisations performed, largely - as we shall argue later - without distortions within particular markets. The relationship of legal structure to legal status should be one where organisations in a given field are permitted to adopt any structure and then compete as they will, but the privileges of status should reflect public policy priorities within any given area, not grant protection to particular organisational forms within them.

Mergers and takeovers

These principles would help to change the role of mergers and takeovers in the non-profit world. Given the rate of creation of new non-profit organisations it is vital that the sector should have easier mechanisms for restructuring, and reorganising and reusing pools of capital which sometimes lie dormant in a trust. At present there are far too many virtually defunct charities, sitting on funds but achieving little.

It should not be the case that the vote of a single trustee is sufficient to veto any proposed merger or takeover. The majorities, weighted or otherwise, required for this should be a matter for each individual organisation to decide when it adopts its governing instruments and should be open to change by later directors. One benefit of a more flexible legal framework would be that it would become possible for bodies themselves to decide how far they will protect themselves, if at all, against takeover. Best practice would probably tend towards a less rigid approach than is currently the norm.

Regulation and control of abuse and fraud

The corollary of greater flexibility is that there will need to be greater accountability and monitoring. The system of oversight for prevention of fraud and abuse in the charitable world, and action when they are detected, is fragmented and poorly co-ordinated. The Charity Commissioners, auditors, the Inland Revenue, Companies House, the police and Crown Prosecution Service all have a role. By contrast the system for for-profit firms is much more streamlined and effective. Removal of the tax-law link would make it possible - indeed necessary - to integrate the financial supervision of all organisations, irrespective of organisational form. Such rigour is essential if the economic weight of the sector is going to continue growing.

Laws and taxation

We have already seen that current tax policy is tightly bound up with legal structure. If an organisation can gain charitable status, it automatically qualifies for tax exemption. The result is that there are odd anomalies and incentives. Some organisations try to squeeze themselves into charitable definitions, whilst others engaged in identical activities are without tax advantages. The link between tax and law also blocks policy debate, since almost any proposals to rethink charity status appears to threaten some vested interest.

Moreover existing policies have peculiar effects. Despite tax exemptions charities are overall a net contributor to the Treasury, primarily because of non-recoverable VAT. The average recovery rate is about 50%, but this falls to 11% for smaller charities. Another anomaly is that rules on commercial activity are routinely broken: although 37% of charity income comes from trading, only a small proportion is earned through subsidiaries, implying that most are in breach of the rules.[38]

By what principles should tax for charitable or other purposes be determined? A variety of principles have been suggested. Some argue that because charity precedes government it should automatically be tax exempt (presumably of all taxes).[39] Others suggest that exemption for charities is justified because of the savings for public spending.[40] Most of these arguments soon run into problems. For example the historical argument is simply incorrect: most modern charity has grown from the same sources as the modern state, and follows state action and encouragement. The argument for substitution raises questions about who should have a legitimate role in deciding which sorts of activities are substitutes for the state's work.

Most assume that generalised tax incentives are effective, and much of recent policy has been premised on the assumption that the 'price' of giving influences its amount. But the evidence available from the US and the UK shows that both the decision to give money at all, and the decision how much to give, are not very sensitive to changes in the 'price': in other words the influence of tax relief.[41] The widespread economists' belief in the 1980s that each pound spent on tax relief for donors would elicit more than a pound of charitable giving is no longer tenable. This is particularly true in the UK where not much giving is tax exempt (covenants, payroll giving and large gifts), and where even these exemptions have had little visible effect on overall giving. Nor is it obvious that generalised tax exemptions help redistribution of resources from the rich to the poor. It is probably more likely that the rich will give more to charitable schools, opera houses and the like than they give to pro-poor charities. There are similar problems with other arguments. The best known argues that non-profit organisations are constrained in their ability to raise capital, because they cannot issue equity shares, or offer equity as collateral against which to raise loan capital. This has considerable substance. But this problem might be better addressed through specific approaches to investments in charity (as we suggest in the following section) rather than through generalised subsidies which may also cover such things as advertisements and salaries in a charity.

Many of the illogicalities of existing tax reliefs, and of their justifications, stem from the tight link between tax and organisational form. We propose a different approach.

Firstly, as we have argued, organisations ought to be free to select the organisational structure they feel most comfortable with, given their members, their field and their interests. The tax system ought not to distort that choice by giving advantages by organisational form.

Society does not gain by organisations choosing one form over another, but rather by what they do.

Secondly, tax advantage should be given for activity rather than organisational form. The tax system should reward the production of certain outputs, irrespective of the form of the organisations that produce them. The outputs that warrant support will vary over time: they may include sociability (thus encompassing everything from music and sports societies), low income housing or care. They should be consistent with the other activities supported through the tax system. In other words there should be a list of tax exempt or partially exempt outputs and activities for which organisations, irrespective of their form, should be eligible. In tax terms there would be no need for a distinct notion of charity at all.

At present tax exemption and advantages are given to everything from housing to venture capital, private health insurance to pensions. A revised approach might more overtly target issues which are deemed charitable: for example the provision of social housing, drugs rehabilitation, or education.

Such an approach would represent a very major shift. In the shortrun we acknowledge that the current contradictory system is likely to survive. In the next section we therefore set out a series of reforms which would be achievable even without a full scale rationalisation of tax and law.

Rethinking private money

We have described some of the underlying virtues and predispositions towards generosity, sociability, and changemaking. We have highlighted the danger of a financial squeeze forced by the combination of the effects of the National Lottery and the stagnation of the other main sources of money. In this section we describe how to reconnect people's ethical dispositions to money, suggesting a wide range of policy measures including voluntary taxes, new financial institutions focused on the charitable sector, new incentives for investment in charities and other players in the social economy, and the roles of, respectively, individuals, firms and government.

Private generosity

Individuals can show their generosity in a number of ways. They can give outright by donating, where their subsequent involvement can be minimal. They can also give by accepting varying degrees of risk - investing, guaranteeing or loaning money, accepting a potential loss and a lower than commercial rate of interest.

There, is in other words, a continuum between straightforward gifts and commercial investment, rather than a clear dividing line.

The principles of relationship funding

The quality of the gift or investment relationship
determines involvement and outcomes. It shapes the
commitment of the giver or lender, their understanding
of the purposes of the organisation and the time horizons
of their involvement. Qualitative relationships can occur
with any form of finance. But donations will tend to
involve less of a relationship.

How does one create better quality relationships and
greater commitment? There is a considerable literature -
predominantly from the USA - on the principles of
funding. What underlies these principles is the
recognition that charities are not just producers of public
goods. They also embody relationships between the
funder and the receiver. This is part of their value, and,
interestingly, one of the ways in which they may be
becoming closer to the corporate forms of the future if, as
some forecast, there is a slow drift to greater employee
involvement and towards forming 'clubs' out of
customers like Costco, or the many membership schemes
such as those of British Airways.

Charity funding has also been evolving in this way by
nurturing more enduring relationships than the
traditional one-off gift: from affinity cards to Give as You
Earn these involve an engaged emotional relationship. To
bring charitable forms and incentives into line with the
changing culture there may now be a case for developing
new principles to underpin the fiscal regime for charities.
There is a need to encourage more direct relationships
between provider and receiver based on continuing
donations, mentoring, sponsorship, covenant or
investment for a public good purpose, where the line
between self-interest and public interest may be less
sharp.

The situation today

At present despite quite generous new tax incentives the
public remains profoundly confused both about the array
of incentives available and the range of different charities

and voluntary organisations operating. Nor do charities themselves have a clear idea of what is available. A recent Chapter One Group survey noted '..... most charities were unaware of the opportunities offered by direct debits and covenants.......and medium and small sized charities were remarkably ill-informed about the implications of the Charity Act.' As a result, although 32% of the income of the largest charities is covered by tax breaks, less than 10% of the income of smaller charities is. Most personal funding remains spontaneous, unplanned and uncovered by tax exemptions and thus any new financial infrastructure needs to take that into account and be simple to operate.

Media schemes to benefit charity inevitably focus on those bigger charities with name recognition and greater popularity. Banking concessions also tend to favour the larger charities. This is well trodden ground and familiar to those working with small companies. Various ideas have been suggested to remedy these biases, including skewing pooled funds like the National Lottery towards smaller charities or setting a percentage requirement on public contracts to go to smaller charities, as is the case with small business access to government contracts in the USA.

New forms of investment

A range of different types of organisation is now experimenting with new forms of ethically focused investment. These include:

- Organisations such as Mercury Provident, ICOF, the Ecological or Catholic Building Societies that embody non-market principles, that apply social or environmental criteria, and that give depositors a choice about where investments should go, and about the interest rate they wish to charge.
- Commercial companies where an ethical concern is an important aspect of their work; for example ethical investment funds such as Friends Provident or Jupiter,

Tyndall, Merlin, who screen their investments according to a range of criteria, typically excluding investment in armaments, tobacco, alcohol or gaming. Commercial trading companies that only deal in products that are produced in what are deemed to be non-exploitative ways, are environmentally friendly or assist local employment initiatives. Traidcraft or Cafedirect are examples. These are able to charge an 'ethical premium' for their goods and services.

● Geographically based organisations such as credit unions, which provide a means of saving and borrowing for their members in a given locality. There are 377 credit unions in Britain with total assets of £23.5 million. Their reduced rates of interest allow their members, who would not receive loans from traditional sources, to raise credit.

Untapped resources and the relative success of ethical investment
These bodies are pioneering a new landscape. But there is still much more money that could be tapped for ethical and charitable purposes. As we have seen individual donations lie somewhere between £4.8 and £6.7bn per annum. Ethical investment funds have now reached £800 - 900 million and have been growing at a compound rate of 35% per annum; ethically screened investments by churches, charities and local authority investment funds using PIRC's socially responsible investment services expands the universe of 'ethical funds' to approaching £45bn. There is also scope to increase this even further. Funds holding charitable investments are estimated to be around £30bn, of which only a small proportion are invested with ethical purposes in mind.

Just as it is wrong to see charity solely in terms of sacrifice, so is it wrong to see crude tradeoffs between ethics and profit. Most ethically invested funds perform on average as well as, if not better than mainstream investment. Furthermore the default rates of most alternative investment schemes undertaken by organizations such as Mercury Provident, Regional Arts Boards or credit unions are far lower than in traditional banking. They share this feature with a wide range of mutual forms of investment - from those common amongst small firms Italy to schemes like the Grameen Bank in Bangladesh. Their closeness works as a moral pressure - it improves the assessments of investments, it motivates the recipients to try harder, and it is likely to make the investor more patient. One small example is Mercury Provident which started in 1974 and has only had two defaults.

So far, however, the mainstream financial institutions have been surprisingly reticent about applying their ingenuity to this field. Every week several hundred new financial products are launched on the market, to help with hedging, or to achieve flexibility with personal pensions or mortgages. Many are evolving towards greater individual control and transparency. But there are none on offer which make links, between, for example, personal motivations and an investment programme in an inner city area, or for a particular cause (for example building foyers). Strangely, personal engagement and risk appear to be more acceptable in the case of specialist funds investing in emerging markets than for specialist funds investing in social needs.

Strategic initiatives

To create a base for financial research and development, and for implementing new mechanisms, we need a stronger set of institutions and incentives to give overall direction to charitable giving and investment.

A bank with charitable purpose and understanding
We start with institutions because ethical money remains underserved by institutions. The priority now is to develop a new bank or set of banks, based upon the kind of principles that Mercury Provident/Triodos operates. Its establishment would reinforce the developing financial expertise in the sector. There is a powerful political argument for its establishment, as well as that of a merchant bank, if there is to be a level playing field

between the commercial, charitable and voluntary sector.

The most recent attempt to create a bank was The Charity Bank idea sponsored by CAF which fell foul of regulators in late 1993. The bank sought to provide investment funding for major charitable projects, to provide loans for charities with liquidity problems and to provide financial advice and services tailored to charities needs. With an asset base of £35 million it would have sought investments and deposits from the private sector and individuals. Part of the initial equity it was hoped would come from the National Lottery. Significantly as an operating bank it widened the definition of collateral as a means of maximising depositors and lenders potential. This included 'specialist receivables' such as payments due on contracts from the European Union, the government or local authorities, tax recoveries due or trustee guarantees.

The Bank of England was unwilling to give its blessing. It felt that CAF had an insufficient track record, and that the charitable sector was too homogenous, breaching the rules about limiting investments to 15% in any sector (a rather odd ruling given the wide range of sectors in which charity is involved). They did not believe that CAF had sufficient resources either to carry out an expansion of activities or to deal with losses.

The Bank of England's objections were based on its legal obligation to licence banks, in order to protect the public who place deposits with them. Commercial banking takes in the public's savings and guarantees their safety through capital reserves and collateral on loans. We can see the Bank of England's problem with a charity bank. It is hard to see how it would obtain the necessary level of reserves, while collateral is what most charities tend to lack. However none of these objections turns out to be that robust on inspection. In the first place the charities now have very large reserves and assets. In the second the record of investment in charities and alternative funds suggests that it can match financial security with other kinds of guarantee.

Interestingly, the regulators may soon lose control over these new forms of banking. With the single European market it is now possible to register a bank in another European country, such as Holland, with less restrictive rules, and so allow banks sympathetic to the sector to be set up on the lines of the Dutch Triodos Bank.

A Charity Merchant Bank
Russell Sparkes in his Demos report[42] suggested a charity merchant bank as another alternative. It would, like other merchant banks, live on its wits rather than by providing capital. Merchant banks - which need not be registered banks - have two main functions: corporate finance, and fund management. Corporate finance includes advice on fund-raising, mergers and acquisitions, project finance, and asset sales. Fund management, as well as being highly profitable, as the fees of £150 million earned by fund managers on charitable investment accounts show, also gives the merchant bank additional clout when it comes to fund-raising (subject to fiduciary duty of course).

A specialist charity merchant bank would work in an innovative way to help individual social economy organisations, and be paid fees for its work. Such a charity merchant bank has a number of distinct advantages. By not taking in deposits from the public it would not need a banking licence, or a high level of reserves. Its legal structure would be flexible, and it could be established as a friendly society or a company limited by guarantee, for example. Essentially it would act as an specialist intermediary between the worlds of commerce and finance, and the voluntary sector. It would be what Mark Lattimer of the Directory of Social Change has called: 'the Holy Grail of the social economy - a source of development finance for charities and other non-profit making organisations which is commercially justifiable'.

How might it work? Suppose a private firm and a voluntary body are both in competition for a hospital cleaning contract, for which specialist equipment is required. If they are equal in other respects, the fact that the commercial company can get cheap finance from the capital markets denied to the charity gives the former a big advantage. The Government via the Private Financial Initiative is increasingly looking to joint ventures between the public/private sectors to fund a range of projects; a merchant bank could be proactive in bringing projects of this type forward for consideration with the involvement of voluntary organisations. It might also act as a home for brokering social investment - a base for the type of imaginative initiative being undertaken around the world by the Social Venture Network.

There is probably room ultimately for several such charity merchant banks. There could be two linked to the NCVO and CAF, another focused on housing associations, one concentrated on community development linked to local authorities, and lastly one deriving from an existing social 'bank' such as Mercury Provident. Of all these, CAF has come furthest. One of the keys to merchant banking is the ability to put together effective packages quickly. CAF for example has a charitable loan service, with experience of project finance such as packaging a number of late grants from the EU into a £12m TSB bridging loan.

Another key attribute is to be innovative and proactive. Charities lose millions through the fear and ignorance of many donors. The launch in September 1994 by CAF of the Charity Card addressed this problem, as it suddenly made available a low cost and flexible way to donate to charity and reclaim 25% tax.

Advice on possible linkages with the commercial sector is another function - this could be targeted advice to a particular charity regarding a commercial company, again on a fee-paying basis if the project is successful. Just as CAF's loan service sifts and polishes loan applications, so that the ones which reach the banks have a high probability of success, so this service could use its knowledge and database of charity need and commercial track record to produce a far more focused and effective package.

Voluntary taxation

The examples above focused on investment, but what about gifts? At present charities benefit from small tax exemptions for gifts, as well as from contracts financed out of general taxation. A far more radical option is to use the tax system to direct funds straight into charities rather than in the form of government contracts. Historically tax developed as a state monopoly, and any suggestions of opening tax out to other players are usually ruled out of court. But there are many examples of more flexible approaches: the taxes for service boards in the 19th century, the taxes paid to churches in Germany on a voluntary basis, the saving banks - the 'caixa' - in Spain which require a proportion of profits to go to charity and voluntary organisations, and the various earmarked taxes that are familiar in the USA. There is no intrinsic reason why the complex infrastructures of taxation need to raise funds only for the state.

Using the hugely sophisticated tax system to generate funds for independent agencies could significantly increase giving and help finance many socially useful activities which cannot be funded easily out of tax revenues, because of public resistance to compulsory taxation and distrust of government as an agent for achieving social goals.

How would voluntary taxation work? We suggest a variety of mechanisms:

The opt in tranche

On the national level, income tax forms could offer an opt-in tranche of monies - perhaps 2% of the total - to be allocated to nominated charities. There would be an option not to pay this tranche. The Inland Revenue would act as a clearing house for payments. The mechanics could take a range of forms: writing in a nominated charity (or code); attaching a code which would be made available by the charities themselves, probably using national newspaper advertisements; selecting a default option (of a general fund, or funds covering a particular sector such as housing or medical research). Inland Revenue tax rebates could as a matter of course offer an option to give a percentage to charity, with the IR providing a service (and taking a small commission) for directing funds to nominated charities.

A parallel option could be on the Council Tax form, with taxpayers again having the option to allocate an additional 2% of their bill to nominated local charities or charitable projects - perhaps up to a given maximum, again with a number of default options.

VAT refunds
Another option would be to initiate a voluntary, that is refundable extra 1% on VAT on purchases over £5, which could be a painless way of raising substantial extra resources in a voluntary manner. For example, the purchaser of a good costing £10 would normally pay an additional 18.5% VAT, of which 1% would go to charity, but would have the option of asking for an immediate refund of the 1% (10p in this case). Collection would be undertaken by Customs and Excise as with VAT. There would be considerable administrative and collection complications with such a scheme but it is an obvious cash analogy to the charity credit card and becomes steadily cheaper as more transactions take the form of electronic debit or credit.

The sums involved could be very large. 2% on income tax would raise £1.4bn; a 2% average premium on council tax would raise nearly £200m. Because they are incremental, small percentages of large numbers (rather like affinity cards) they are a painless way of giving.

From the perspective of those who need money this may be the greatest virtue of voluntary tax. But it also has wider virtues. It reconnects individuals to social goals without the state as sole intermediary. It symbolises a philosophical shift in the role of government, ending its monopoly over fund-raising and opening itself up to civil society.

All of these mechanisms involve new ways of hypothecating funds, making a closer connection between taxes and uses than the current pooling of tax funds to be parcelled out in the form of contracts by national and local government. Some of these ideas are set out in greater detail in the Demos booklet *Reconnecting Taxation*.[43] For example Welsh speakers might seek to earmark their funds to projects involving Welsh-speakers; those who have recovered from a serious illness might earmark their funds to self-help groups organised around that illness.

All are ways of increasing resources while also increasing the independence of the sector. They require shifts both in public policy - particularly in relation to tax and incentives - as well as shifts in the internal culture and organisation of non-profits.But they have a potential to change the culture of giving, introducing a much easier way to raise funds, and symbolising a change in the relationship between the sector and the state from one of dependence to partnership.

Related initiatives to raise new money

Linked to the set of charitable financial institutions, which would over time develop financial packages and products to increase finance for charities, a range of other initiatives should be put in place which largely rely government sanction. They include:

The development of a Charitable Expansion Scheme
Parallel to the now defunct Business Expansion Scheme and the Enterprise Investment Scheme, there has been some discussion of a Charitable Expansion Scheme (CES) for larger charitable projects. The BES was established to fill a perceived gap in investment in start up companies. The original scheme (started in 1981) allowed individuals to invest up to £40,000 per year in qualifying companies; provided the investment stayed in the company for five years they could receive full tax relief on capital gains. Tax incentives were justified by the broader public good

of promoting enterprise.

BES, both in its original form and in its extension to private rented housing, was very successful in raising money, to such an extent that its tax cost hastened its demise. It has also been used for quasi-charitable purposes - one high profile example was the establishment of a BES by the Centre for Alternative Technology.

There is a case for letting the promoters of CES schemes benefit themselves, encouraging active participation in projects such as an investment in a building, say in a deprived area where a non-profit is working, and where a commercial return is only possible through the tax incentive. Greater flexibility in legal forms might be necessary to achieve the full potential of such schemes, such as developing forms of preference share, or stakeholder bonds to encourage direct involvement in the management of a project. These might be particularly suitable for capital projects associated with local charities involved in special needs schools, housing or youth projects. The Treasury's recently expressed interest in providing incentives for loans to venture capital trust funds suggests that there may well be scope for advancing ideas of this kind.

The loan guarantee

A tax incentive for contingent expenditure on guarantees given to charities by third parties could be offered. The Treasury usually shuns bank guarantees. But unofficially the practice is already happening. As most non-profits organisations have few capital assets it is difficult to borrow for expansion or to trade their way out of a crisis. A major asset especially for revenue clients, is next year's grant. A number of funders have been in contact with clients banks to provide letters of comfort (not far short of an official guarantee), which have enabled borrowing limits to be increased. The value of the guarantees of this sort, we have identified, is in the order of several hundred million pounds - its leverage capacity is thus very great.

Trustees of charities already quite regularly provide

Rethinking private money

guarantees. There has also been some experimentation with 'borrowing communities' whereby a group of individuals cross-guarantee a loan from a financial institution which is then turned into a grant to a charity. But a wider group of guarantors could be harnessed both by a possible tax incentive, by thinking of the guarantee itself as a form of 'donation', that may or may not be called upon.

CAF has proposed a National Guarantee Fund, which might tap the foreign banks in the City to guarantee between £2.5m and £5m of loans. This might in turn lever 10 times as much money. There are a number of such guarantee funds elsewhere, such as in Mondragon in the Basque country, which has never had a default. There is also the Queen Juliana Fund linked to the NMB Bank. Initially the fund guaranteed loans given by NMB and the risk was on a 1 to 5 basis, but this has now increased to 1 to 22 and the bank has stated that it no longer requires the Fund as backer.

Loans and bonds
Other popular charitable savings options could be developed with care and good marketing. Capital charity projects could be financed from bond offerings at less than market rates without the lure of a tax break, as Mercury Provident have done. An incentive would help as well as signalling that this is a type of financial instrument that the government wishes to foster. There might be a general charity bond, raised by government or local authorities, or specific bonds could be raised for particular projects requiring an urgent response, like an Africa Bond, potentially offering investors a choice of interest rates. Tax deductibility could be offered on the difference between the interest offered on the bond and the potential return elsewhere. Such bonds could either be specific to charities or provide the underpinning for a Charity Bank, as well as providing loan finance for charities. Bond finance of this kind may also provide a good fit with the needs of some of the new charities: opt-

out schools for example.

Education and housing are good examples of social objectives being linked to the need to raise capital. Social housing, traditionally the province of local authorities, has shifted over the last fifteen years to some 2,200 autonomous housing associations, which now manage 1,000,000 homes or 5% of the total housing stock.

Local authority funds can be used to leverage activity. A creative example was that carried out by the New York City Pension fund, which with $50bn in assets is the second largest in the US. As its former Comptroller Elizabeth Holtzman stated:

'We wanted to invest some of the funds' assets in affordable housing, but were limited in what we could do by fiduciary responsibilities. We discovered that there were federal government mortgage guarantees available to the banks covering 90% of the cost of any investment in designated areas. However, the banks at that time were short of capital, and unwilling to put any of it to this use. What we did was to go to the banks and say that we would supply all the capital required if they would shoulder the risk of the 10% not covered by guarantees. In three years we were able to fund 16,000 units of affordable housing in some of the poorest parts of New York, and did so in such a way that was risk free and generated above average returns, so there could be no argument on fiduciary grounds. So what I would advise British local authorities is to be innovative, be creative, there is often a way through if you look for it.'

There has been creativity in Britain, but more on the side of housing associations. Since the passage of the 1988 Housing Act, some £5.5bn has been raised from the financial markets. £3.9bn was lent by banks and building societies on traditional lines. What is revolutionary is the £1.6bn coming from sales of bonds to institutional investors, with such big investment banks as Hambros, Kleinwort Benson, Nat West Markets, and UBS among the main players. The deals have become increasingly innovative. In November 1994 Sanctuary Housing

Association raised £47.3m by placing a 17 year bond with US private investors in a deal arranged by Hambros Bank, with the loans being repaid from its rental income of £30m a year. At the end of 1994 six small housing associations banded together to form a pooled group called UK Rents and issued a £36.6m Eurobond. Housing associations must be congratulated on finding this additional source of finance. However this does not imply any long-term commitment of financial institutions to the social economy; it is rather that, as the credit rating agency IBCA put it 'housing associations rank with larger property companies and middle ranking building societies as investment opportunities.'

Education is another area where loans and bonds are becoming increasingly important. The 1988 Education Act set a target of increasing the number of students in higher education by 33% in the year 2000. Who is going to pay for this expansion, and in particular for 'capital items' such as new laboratories and expanded libraries? Since the beginning of 1995, both the University of Lancaster and Nottingham Law School have announced plans to raise money via share issues, as has Birmingham.

Lenders in future will need to look at 'social' factors such as reputation, popularity, commitment of staff and the like to ascertain how viable social projects such as universities are going to be over the long-term, as the value of their assets is usually likely to be insufficient. In fact, universities and other social companies may find that relationships develop best with socially responsible investors, which is why the development of charitable banking institutions is so important.

Mutual Funds
Another option for developing charity finance would be to create mutual funds linking the major charities, perhaps in a particular sector like cancer research or disability. The reserves of these charities (which are very substantial in some cases) would then be pooled for onward loans to charities within this sector, with the

assessment done by agents of the funding charities themselves. Funds of this kind should have very low default rates. This would also offer a neat way of using accumulated reserves in ways that would fit better with charitable objects than investment on the stock market. It might even encourage existing banks, or the Bank of England, to follow the Belgian example and establish equity pools for charities and the social economy.

Supporting schemes to increase private generosity

The incidental giving tax break

We have already noted the high preponderance of incidental, unplanned, spontaneous giving. Extending relief to incidental giving would go with the flow of what people prefer to do and their psychologies of involvement. Current schemes are tilted towards the regular giver and the recipient charity. Allowing tax remission to those who make spur of the moment or irregular donations will encourage them, albeit only marginally. A possible mechanism is an automatic allowance of say £200 per annum, claimable against tax on production of a receipt from a charity - a simple and effective device.

Alternatively there could be a voucher system whereby a booklet would be purchased and tax deductibility given for the purchase. The booklet would be used to make donations throughout the year. On balance the allowance scheme may be preferred as it could be coded into PAYE deductions and entered into Schedule D returns. Since it requires no prior decision it is also more likely to increase casual donations.

The small scale endowment

It could be made simpler to create smaller personal endowment funds, with public good purposes as their goal, to encourage the setting up of funds of up to £5,000, which would allow charity to be popularised. Endowments provide givers with the chance to identify themselves more sharply with their giving. These might have purposes such as funding gardens or hospices, new music or improvements to a local public park. This would be a way of letting ethical commitments 'cascade down the generations'. Such funds might be pooled into new types of financial institution - for example a revolving endowment fund raised from sufferers of heart disease that is used to help other sufferers, or more general revolving funds for the elderly. The funds would need simplified trust deeds to reduce set up costs and thus would have to be given a degree of latitude, but given their small size the level of any possible abuse can be contained.

Locally focused initiatives

It is in poor areas that money is most needed. In part more money can be generated through internally developed financial institutions such as credit unions and community banks and in part through feeding in resources from outside.

Revitalizing the community economy

One of the core problems of local development economics is to ensure that money stays in the local community and creates a multiplier effect by being recycled through local shops and financial institutions. Pat Conaty of the Birmingham Settlement (founded in 1899) is seeking to put this principle into practice:

'In a wealthy neighbourhood, money circulates eight to ten times before leaving. In run down, unemployed areas it will be only two or three...to counteract this trend community development organisations have developed the theory of the working neighbourhood. This includes:

● strong purchasing power (i.e. high neighbourhood income)
● numerous locally owned shops
● diversity of local employment and business opportunities
● a range of affordable housing

● cycles of local re-investment'

Pat Conaty set up the Aston Development Trust, which aims to raise £3.5m, to expand on the work of its Money Centre. Local re-investment was impaired by the spate of bank closures in recent years. The Aston Trust is modelled on US community banks which have proved that it is possible to lend to businesses in poor communities on very low loan loss ratios. He is clear about its objectives:

'The system does not want to lend on the strength of character and commitment, but on the basis of money. If you have a good business idea but are a black woman in a tower block, no bank will lend you the money because you don't fit their criteria. Our aim is to lend to people who have good ideas but not a lot of security.'

A study by the University of Strathclyde proves the potential effectiveness of this approach and found that 48 community businesses had created 912 jobs at a capital cost of £4,500 per job. Significantly, 81% of the jobs went to people living in the local community. Compare that with the London Docklands Development Corporation, which announced in September 1994 that it had created 72,000 jobs at a rate of £35,168 per job in its area.

A Local Investment Fund

A related geographical approach is to create Local Investment Funds (LIF), one of which has recently been set up as a matching fund associated with Business in the Community. Its key concept is to find ways in which funders can invest in non-profits as well as make grants and donations. Good examples already exist in Holland and the USA. The government has pledged a one-off initial £1 million with no strings attached, which is effectively an equity input into the fund. This has been matched by £2 million in loans or donations from the private sector. LIF will provide technical advice, training and evaluation, and represents Phase 1 of a two phase project. It is intended as a pilot scheme in narrowly defined geographic areas that will act as a catalyst. Phase

2 will be national in scope.

The second phase would involve a number of authorised deposit-taking institutions with shareholders drawn from corporations active in a region and deposits coming from (mostly individual) 'ethical' depositors. The latter will benefit from the provisions of the Deposit Protection Scheme. If this scheme is successful it will set a stronger basis for the development of community banking in Britain. Its closest equivalent in Britain is Mercury Provident.

A Charitable Enterprise Zone
This is an idea that has been proposed in the Joseph Rowntree Foundation and Anglo-German Foundation sponsored project *Investing in People - Rescuing people from the margin*. This would offer not only certain tax breaks for companies setting up in specific areas of deprivation, but also tax reliefs for charitable activities within that area. CEZ status could be something that a community bids for and the government grants once it has developed a regeneration strategy. The CEZ is one way of acknowledging that the social fabric is usually as important as the physical fabric. Incentives might include tax breaks for secondees or others willing to work in the zone as well as the more traditional means such as breaks for businesses lending premises for charitable purposes.

Such a zone need not only be geographical. It could also be functional, giving specific incentives to deal with particular problems such as community enterprises at a time of rising unemployment. Zones of this kind, although 'distorting' the neutrality of taxes, could be a useful tool of policy. Places like Belfast whose broader regeneration is more likely to involve a wide variety of community initiatives would be particularly appropriate for CEZ status.

Area based affinity cards
Affinity cards tend to benefit the better known charities. However their principles could be extended to help

specific areas. This might be done by offering a card that ploughs back money into a named area such as Easterhouse, which could for example appeal to Bank of Scotland cardholders living near the area. The second option is to create an affinity card for an issue (such as homelessness) which is then distributed between large and small charities.

Affinity cards are a good example of the way entrepreneurial charities are working with the financial sector to mutual benefit. A sign of their popularity is that they are the only area of credit card usage which is growing - the total number of credit cards in issue having declined since a peak in 1989. The TCB extended its range of affinity cards in October 1993 when it added Amnesty International to its affinity card list. Amnesty gets £5 for every new account opened, and 20p for every £100 spent. The Co-operative Bank now has 5 affinity cards. The two Scottish banks (Bank of Scotland introduced affinity cards into the UK in 1988), and the Co-operative Bank are the major players in the field of affinity cards.

Affinity cards have worked very well for some charities. The Leeds Permanent's card has raised £4m for its group of three charities, while the largest amount received by a single charity card was over £1m for the card issued by the Co-operative Bank for the Royal Society for the Protection of Birds. The benefits are not just financial; as well as generating a steady stream of income, affinity cards can extend the donor base through free publicity. Charities with mass memberships can promote them as a service to supporters, and receive extra income through tied-in deals on insurance and pensions. However, it must also be added that for the sector as a whole it is small beer, with CAF statistics showing that affinity cards contribute less than 0.5% of donation income a year.

Business generosity and the ethical premium

The new corporate philanthropy
We have described new forms of personal giving and investment. What of the firm? In Britain as elsewhere there is a long history of corporate generosity. It has been marked in firms with a Quaker connection, and firms with strong family ownership: obvious examples include Sainsbury's, Cadbury Schweppes and Marks and Spencer.

Strategists have identified three waves in the evolution of corporate community involvement. The first typically involves small amounts of cash giving on an ad hoc basis, largely at the whim of the company chairman. The 'second wave' sees companies adopt a more sophisticated approach, setting aside an annual budget and establishing an in-house department for community affairs. According to Business in the Community, its leading companies have now advanced to the 'third wave' which involves the complete integration of community affairs with business objectives.

This 'new corporate philanthropy' has been pioneered by firms like AT&T, IBM and ARCO the aim being to use giving to help increase a company's name recognition among consumers, develop and widen employees' interests and skills, improve internal corporate communication and morale, influence government, and even to reduce research and development costs. Some of the leading corporate donors, such as Shell, National Westminster Bank, British Petroleum and British Telecom, now only support community activities where they perceive the business rationale for doing so. Companies like Volkswagen and General Accident, for example, have switched their spending on the arts and sport to support road-safety campaigns and crime-prevention organisations respectively. This is clearly intended to develop a closer link between the company's donations and its products. By conveying an impression of corporate social responsibility in the market place, each business now uses philanthropy or 'social sponsorship' to try to steal a march on its competitors.

Companies today are defining their community as a large and heterogeneous group; no longer restricted to a relatively small number of directors, investors and senior management who are primarily interested in short-term performance and profit. The corporate community now extends to include the company's employees and their dependants; the neighbourhoods and towns which surround a firm's locations; suppliers and business partners, and increasingly well-informed customers who are often as interested in a firm's contribution to the quality of life, as in the quality of its product.

More than merely money

On paper the corporate role remains relatively small. Only a few charities receive significant funding from business; Cancer Relief MacMillan Fund (27% in 1992/93), Charity Projects/Comic Relief (25%) and Barnardos (16%), Overall levels of UK corporate giving are barely one fifth of those of US corporations. But this may overlook the different nature of social intervention by the respective private sectors. In the US 85% of corporate giving is in cash. The figure is only 60% in the UK. As one community affairs manager has remarked 'if you concentrate on company giving you are missing 90 per cent of companies' potential to manage change.'

In Britain the most significant form of non-cash giving is the deployment of staff resources. Companies like Allied Dunbar, Kingfisher and Whitbread, which have extensive employee involvement schemes, cite a range of benefits to their companies including improvements in organisational culture, staff motivation and morale as well as public relations. Intermediary organisations like the volunteer bureaux and Action: Employees in the Community exist to help match employees with appropriate voluntary organisations. The government has also indicated its commitment through the 'Make a Difference' campaign to build up the volunteer infrastructure in the UK.

Linking community benefit to commercial goals
One of the best examples is Allied Dunbar, which gives more than £2.5m a year, with three distinct grant making trusts. The AD Foundation is a general charity, raising most of its money from donations from its sales force, who therefore determine what its areas of support should be: in 1994/95 it was the family, with grants made to projects in areas like homelessness, mental illness, hospices, and disability. The Staff Charity Fund raises funds from staff matched by donations from the Charitable Trust concentrating on needs round the head office in Swindon. The AD Charitable Trust is funded by the company, receiving 1.25% of pretax profits, with grants of £1.5m in 1993. The Charitable Trust sees itself as a 'Collaborative Entrepreneur':

"We seek out charities we would like to work with within the policy areas we have chosen to support, and longer-term relationships are developed in which both parties work together. ....We plan a long-term and focused commitment. '

The Trust's approach is refreshing in that it concentrates on long-term funding of staffing costs rather than capital projects. Projects in 1994 included support for carers, money advice (including significant funding of debt counsellors in Citizens Advice Bureaux) and domestic violence.

Companies are developing a variety of ways of linking charitable and self-interested goals. One cost-effective way to provide childcare is for a company to develop locally-provided services which meet its requirements at the same time as providing a much needed community service and creating some employment. Corporations which have gone down this road include the Prudential in Reading, where the company subsidises local crêche facilities, and American Express which has established a database network of approved childminders in Brighton, its UK headquarters.

Business support for a community's education facilities can generate research and development spin-offs. Glaxo, the pharmaceutical company which is building a new Medicines Research Centre in Stevenage, had this in mind when it recently donated £285,000 to improve the chemistry and biology facilities of nearby North Hertfordshire College. American Express has helped to design aspects of the new GCSE curricula for travel and tourism courses which it hopes will help to dispel the image of the industry as one of low-skilled, low-paid occupations.

Numerous companies draw on their community involvement or social awareness for marketing purposes. Whitbread, for instance, have recently rewritten their graduate recruitment literature in order to emphasise their record of corporate citizenship. Allied Dunbar found that recruitment posters which publicised the firm's community involvement generated four times as many responses as those which did not. Other marketing is intentionally more discreet. Wellcome, the pharmaceutical giant and producer of the controversial HIV/Aids treatment AZT had a vested interest in supporting the work of the Terence Higgins Trust.

Community involvement and corporate identity
Corporate community affairs can also bring cohesion and

identity to an otherwise loose-knit organisation. Both the Body Shop and McDonalds UK, for example, use campaigns and charitable work in order to provide several hundred independent franchises with a common cause. The Body Shop ensures that the commitment of prospective business partners to the company's community programmes is a prerequisite of acquiring a franchise. Head office's part of the bargain is to help to resource the activity of the stores.

Most companies also use their work in the community to win influence with government. This occurs at local, national and international level. Boots and Marks and Spencer, for example, are frequently involved in inner-city and town-centre initiatives in partnership with voluntary organisations and local authorities. These contacts can prove useful in the event of having to influence a local planning enquiry. Both British Midland and British Airways are active supporters of the Community Development Foundation (CDF), a national charity funded by the Home Office. The current chairman of CDF is a Member of Parliament on the House of Commons Transport Select Committee.[44] In Brussels when lobbying the European Commission on the Directive for the Protection of Young People at Work, Burger King (a subsidiary of Grand Metropolitan) cited its investment in their young employees, including inner-city education projects, in a failed attempt to narrow the focus of the legislation to the under-16 age group.

As these examples illustrate, corporate philanthropy can generate numerous benefits to the community, but its primary purpose is to sustain the company. On occasions, and when pressed, few corporations hesitate from using their work in community affairs if it offers a means of legitimising corporate power. In this sense, though, there may be less difference with personal giving than is often acknowledged: both entail exchange.

Pressures for companies to get involved
There are also other pressures. One recent survey of its

typical customer base in Europe commissioned by Levi Strauss and Co. (a family-owned business with a strong reputation for social responsibility) found that a high percentage of the 5000 young people interviewed believe that corporations have a role to play in tackling social issues. This ranged from an affirmative response of 74% in Belgium to 90% in France and Finland. It remains unlikely that this degree of interest will be translated into a commensurate level of discriminating purchasing decisions. The Newcastle-based organisation New Consumer which is devoted to raising people's awareness of their power as consumers, estimates that about 0.5 per cent of all shoppers can be classified as activists and genuinely 'shop for a better world'. Nevertheless, up to 3 million people in the UK (8% of adult consumers) from time to time either purchase or boycott products based on a company's social or environmental record. The Mintel organisation puts this figure far higher. It estimates that 22% of the British public are 'strongly ethical' and prepared to avoid products and companies which they perceive to be irresponsible.

Other research has found that consumers are more comfortable with corporate social involvement where it has clear business as well as community benefits. Activities which smack of pure altruism engender public suspicions of ulterior motives, such as companies dodging taxes, or chairmen pursuing knighthoods.

Community involvement and the bottom line
Companies must always watch their bottom line, so it is no surprise that many have embraced the opportunity to be seen to be doing good, at the same time as boosting profits. During 1992 and again in 1993 Tesco Supermarkets ran a Computers for Schools campaign. For every £25 spent in Tesco's, customers received a voucher which could be exchanged by a school of their choice for Acorn computer equipment. Top of the range systems required 5,000 vouchers (a mere £125,000 worth of groceries); a basic software package could be obtained for

200. Eight thousand schools shared almost £3 million worth of material. Yet the campaign was criticised in some quarters because cash-strapped schools were pressurising parents into shopping in order to obtain the much-needed equipment. Although Tesco has remained coy about the benefits to the company, the figures speak for themselves. It can be assumed that the retailer would not have run a second phase of the campaign unless it had been certain of the benefits to the business.

In spite of the recent proliferation of cause-related marketing, there are signs that companies will find it increasingly difficult to profit by association with a charity or social cause. Both WH Smith and Boots received as much adverse as favourable publicity following their products for schools promotions. WH Smith's Free Books for Schools required customers to submit vouchers in exchange for books. On average each book required £58 to be spent in Smith's stores. Boots was later forced to halve the amount of vouchers which it required before donating 'free' sports equipment to schools. Proctor and Gamble caused a loud outcry in 1993 from the green lobby when it struck a deal with the National Childbirth Trust. In return for a £250,000 donation, the Trust agreed to endorse Pampers , Proctor and Gamble's popular, but environmentally-unfriendly disposable nappies. The company subsequently launched a direct mail campaign to advertise its nappies and to disclaim that they damaged the environment. The letter began 'The National Childbirth Trust recommends Pampers for drier, happier babies.' P&G which holds over half of the UK's £350 million disposable nappy market has seen a £35m increase in turnover since the endorsement.

Some of these schemes engender cynicism. But there is undoubtedly a significant minority of businesses which are deliberately cultivating an ethical orientation which they translate into a premium on prices. Firms like the Body Shop, Ben and Jerry's (which donates 7.5 percent of annual pre-tax profits to charity), the Co-operative Bank and Chateau de Lastours, are carving out new niches which in time are likely to grow. What is interesting about them is the way in which they disprove the idea that there is a trade-off between ethics and good business by tapping into the moral senses of their customers.

Code of conduct - 'Investors in the Community'
Are there any policy conclusions to be drawn from this discussion? People have grown accustomed to the use of Citizens Charters and awards for standards of excellence. These establish a minimum acceptable level of public services and recognise high achievement among businesses in everything from their investment in people to the quality of their products. Business in the Community has long published guidelines for corporate community involvement, but they are neither well enough known, nor very often followed. 'Investors in the Community' (like the 'Investors in People' certification) would be an independently-awarded mark of a socially-responsible corporation, one which fulfilled its dual role as creator of capital and contributor to the community.

Funding public goods

What then of the third major source of funds, government? Before addressing in detail how government should fund, and by what criteria, we need to stand back and consider what it is that governments are funding. Funding for voluntary organisations is just one part of governments funding of the production of public goods. This has been influenced by broader trends: for example the growing use of contracts; the shift towards payment for specified outputs; the formalisation of voluntary activities; the use of vouchers or indirect funding.

But the issues raised go far deeper than these administrative reforms. They involve precisely what we mean by public goods, how they are defined, and how they should be paid for.

Current debate has been intellectually dominated by economic thinking. In the view of economists the essential feature of a public good is its 'non-excludability', that is its provision automatically benefits a wider public and cannot be restricted to personal benefit. Roads, railways, defence and environmental clear ups are some examples.

Secondly, the debate has been dominated by the state: the assumption that wherever there is evidence of a public good there is a role for government to intervene.

We want to question both of these restrictions. The recent fashion in economics has been to narrow the economic definition of public goods on the grounds that non-excludability is often a result of failure to define property rights, that is ownership or user rights, adequately. In the case of roads for example, there are only public goods where there is a failure to develop proper charging mechanisms for road users.

We believe that there are stronger grounds for widening definitions. Many types of activity bring benefits far beyond those directly concerned - and this is certainly the case with many charities, such as those engaged in counselling, care or education. The problem is to define these values precisely. Experience has shown this to be extremely hard. It depends, moreover, on making valuations of other peoples benefits. The difficulties involved have become particularly clear in the environmental field where economists have tried to put values on everything from wetlands to endangered species.

What these bring out is that any coherent conception of public goods necessarily involves the public in making valuations. Some assume that the political system is adequate to this task, through the deliberations of local councils and parliaments. But most available evidence shows that the public does not share this confidence and that instead there is a clear demand for more engagement in decisions, and more scope for direct influence.

How this issue is resolved has huge implications for nonprofit organisations insofar as they depend for their funding on government.

If we accept that there can be a more open definition of public goods and public goals, then the non-profits have essentially two roles. The first is as discovery mechanisms, identifying new needs and new areas of activity. These may include the needs of sufferers from Aids drug dependants, or job creation for 16 year old men.

Their second role is as providers. Few now believe that

the state should have a monopoly over providing public goods. Yet despite having contracted out the provision of many services, governments still retain a close control over the specification of goals.

We would define a public good not only as something the government defines, but also something the public are prepared to make a sacrifice for, to give something up for because they define it as 'good' where there is no direct immediate benefit. As such what a public good is depends on judgement, which in turn has a strong moral component. Furthermore public goods can concern intangible factors such as the morale of a society or social cohesion.

The need for new indicators
How could governments cope with this expanded notion of public goods? The answer lies in the more imaginative use of indicators. There is a long history of attempts to capture what economists call 'externalities': cost benefit analysis, programming planning and budgeting systems (PPBS) for example. Recent years have brought an explosion of new indicators and measurements in the public sector. But the response has not always been positive. As Daniel Yankelovich, the renowned American pollster put it: 'The first step is to measure whatever can be easily measured. This is okay as far as it goes. The second step is to disregard that which can't be measured or give it an arbitrary quantitative value. This is artificial and misleading. The third step is to presume what can't be measured isn't really important. This is blindness. The fourth step is to say that what can't be easily measured really doesn't exist. This is suicide!'

Achieving a more sensible framework requires incorporating qualitative as well as quantitative measures, that capture people's sense of well-being as well as throughputs of services. Psychologists have long known that social factors are essential to happiness and to health: the quality of social relationships, friendships and family.

107

The raw material for a more sophisticated set of indices is emerging out of the work of economists and environmentalists dissatisfied with the crude orthodox measures of wealth and progress. Much of this work originally focused on environmental indicators, but increasingly social, health and cultural indicators are being developed to assess questions such as community spirit or urban vitality. In the US there is now a Civic Index, an Index of Social Health, the Green Index, and the Liveability Index of American Communities developed by Partners for Liveable Communities. In parallel, the World Health Organisation as part of its healthy cities movement has created a similar index. In the UK the New Economics Foundation (NEF) in collaboration with the Stockholm Environment Institute created an Index of Sustainable Economic Welfare, which established that Britain had become poorer over the last decade, if environmental factors are also considered and quantified. Most recently in the aftermath of the Rio Summit six local authorities - Mendip, Merton, Fife, Cardiff, Oldham and Hertfordshire - have joined together to pilot a 'Sustainability Indicators' project as part of their contribution to Local Agenda 21.

One of the crucial features of these new indicators is that unlike a previous generation of indicators devised top-down by government departments they have deliberately involved the public and the voluntary sector in their definition. In other words they are open; they do not pretend to reflect some incontestable reality, but rather combine objective and subjective factors in order to improve government decision-making.

The best of these draw on a wide array of sources: the main statutory sources of statistics, including in particular the *Census of Population*, the *Annual Census of Production*, the *General Household Survey* and the *Family Expenditure Survey* plus others noted in the *Guide to Official Statistics*, provide a baseline which much commercially driven data elaborates upon and extends. In some cases however, nationally available data on say 'walk to work' patterns can be used as a proxy to help measure issues like a sense of local community. Equally data collected for specific purposes include the credit rating data gathered by organisations such as CCN, can be adapted and reinterpreted according to different guidelines.

Perhaps the most important innovation over the last decade has been the development of geographical information systems (GIS) initiated to assess social deprivation. Allied to increased computer power, they allow a much sharper focus on what is happening at postcode enumeration district level. These systems provide a much more sophisticated classification than the traditional socio-demographic categorisations such as the ABC1 definition of the population that throw up all kinds of anomalies.

GIS information providers and handlers are currently developing data on softer attitudinal aspects of our lives, which help assess the health of a community. These include the lifestyle questions of Target Group Index, extensions to the National Shoppers Survey, which taps 1,500,000 people, and already asks questions, for example, about charitable giving, as well as psychographic information gathered by organisations such as AC Synergy. Psychographic profiling of the population seeks to establish the value systems of citizens and how this relates to both consumer choices as well as attitudes to community and family, politics, change and innovation.

But impressive as this public and private data is, it is not enough to capture the fine grain of what is happening at local level, such as how many trees there are or incidences of graffiti. Locally gathered data is essential. It is here, too, that the voluntary sector has to play a central part in monitoring the condition of their localities, whether this involves school children counting frogs as a measure of the pollution of a given area; monitoring levels of conversation on the high street as a measure of sociability; counting the proportions of buildings that are accessible to the disabled; assessing the state of parklands.

The importance of benchmarking

The relevance of such indicators is that they make it possible to imagine very different funding relationships between government and voluntary organisations. Instead of simply contracting to provide a certain number of residential beds, or to treat a specified number of drug addicts, it is possible to provide funding tied to a range of less direct indices: ones related to the quality of social life and relationships for example. Ideally these should be turned into benchmarks for particular communities: shared goals and targets to be achieved, with an open process of consultation to define them. The benchmarks developed by the Oregon Progress Board as a report to the 1991 State Legislature, which aimed to shape Oregon's progress to the year 2010 are perhaps the most well known. Of interest is the fact that the benchmarks were evolved through a process of state-wide meetings, revision and public review involving citizens, experts, business and voluntary groups which enabled citizens to think about the future in concrete and quantifiable terms. They will be continuously revised and updated and become a 'document'. Some examples from the Oregon Benchmarks 1991 are: reducing teen pregnancies from 25 per 100 women between 10-17 in 1980 to 8 by the year 2000; increasing the births of drug free babies from 89% in 1990 to 100% by the year 2000; increasing air quality standards to meet government guidelines by 1995 and reducing crime rates by 10% every five years.

From the selection of indicators it can be seen how important the role of the voluntary sector will be in achieving targets. The Oregon benchmarks set a new standard for world best practice and are being replicated elsewhere, including the Minnesota's Milestones; Life in Jacksonville; Quality Indicators for Progress; Quality of Life Indicators for Metro Kansas City.

Their ultimate promise is of a much more open public sector - open to influences about priorities, open to partnerships on how to achieve them and open to spending public money on the basis of those influences.

110

Public Money

Public funding is, after earned income, the largest source of charitable and voluntary sector income (at 35-39%). For many organizations, as in the rest of the world, it remains the main income source.

However, public spending is constrained for many reasons: tax resistance, upward cost pressures (particularly in labour intensive services), new demands (such as for long-term care). These result in pressures to squeeze more out of existing funds - one reason why the contract culture is unlikely to go away.

Beyond the giving of one-off grants and contracts, by what principles should governments fund the non-profit sector to maximize its impact? The great fear of most non-profits is that state funding compromises their independence. This is clearly the case with the contract culture: the purchaser is able to specify the nature of the service and becomes the primary line of accountability. In itself this is not obviously wrong since the government has a duty to use public resources responsibly and to attach strings to them. However, with a proper indicators process in place, which involves the broader public in its definition so that it meets real needs, funding could be used more imaginatively to support a sector better able to fund itself and to increase local capacities. Much is already happening around the use of focus groups, benchmarks, neighbourhood councils and the like.

But few of these have yet affected the forms of money to cultivate a better quality of money - that is money which is better fitted to what it is funding, and money that better achieves value. Achieving this might involve some of the following features, which combine greater flexibility and partnership on the one hand and greater rigour in specifying targets on the other:

● The offer of matching funds, as happens in the case of disaster relief, as an incentive for charitable fund-raising. The matching funds idea could also kickstart some of our proposals, such as creating a Loan Guarantee

111

Fund or Charity Bank.

- General purpose partnership funding based more on the idea of trust, with triggers for review, in place of contractual funding. This would imply providing core funding, for instance, to a housing charity, with regular oversight based on broader performance measures rather than tying funds specifically to quantifiable outcomes. This has already occurred, for example, in relation to the NCVO which administers European Social Fund resources on behalf of central government.
- Partnership finance in the form of overt mixed equity stakes in a project with clear time-horizons and joint control. Again, government could collaborate on the establishment of a new housing project with an initial equity stake and participation in decision-making as an alternative to reliance on revenue funding. Such stakes could gradually diminish to be replaced by revenue finance.
- The development of local or regional bonds taking advantage of local loyalties, offering below commercial returns to finance an investment, perhaps in housing or an environmental project.These could be guaranteed by local government but tap into individual commitments.
- Steadily increasing the proportion of contracts which involve overt assessments by users, particularly for charitable work where the key benefits involve the subjective well-being of groups such as the terminally ill or people with disabilities.

Public funders should systematically use benchmarking to discover relative inefficiencies, and their sources. An interesting example is the preliminary study done for the Australian Industry Commission on Charitable Organisations by London Economics. This analysed a number of Australian NGOs to show where there was scope for operational improvement.

Provision of services needs to be linked to formalised accreditation models for quality, involving peer review with assessors, and quality systems that involve feedback from clients. The UK has been quite advanced in adopting quality standards (eg the adoption of ISO 9000 series in health care), and should continue improving and refining the relevant definitions of quality.

A new balance between flexibility and accountability needs to evolve. It will depend on certain potentially difficult issues being resolved: potential obligations arising from matching funding commitments; greater flexibility for local government to match voluntarily provided funds; a willingness to share control over joint projects; a greater flexibility in terms of the contingent liabilities potentially created by government involvement in bonds. They require an acceptance by government that it needs partnerships, trust and flexibility to maximise the production of public goods, and an acceptance from charities that they need to be open to scrutiny. But the reward for both would be a more effective partnership in solving problems.

Engaging government

We have described a wide range of different types of
policy initiative to give new shape and energy to the non-
profit sector. Many would involve changes to law, to tax
policy and to the shape and rules attached to public
funding.

But what should be governments' overall relation to
ethically-motivated actions of the kind we have described?
And what institutional links should there be?

Some have made the case for a centralised point of
contact between government and the voluntary sector: a
new ministry, a specialised part of the Cabinet Office (as
the Voluntary Services Unit originally was), a high profile
Cabinet committee, perhaps a new base in the
Department of the Environment or yet another national
quango to coordinate community schemes. All of these
might achieve some short-term gains. But they rather
miss the point.

Over the years ahead what is today a coherent sector
will become ever less so. The connections between
housing organisations, drugs treatment organisations and
charities involved in overseas aid will become even looser.
What government needs is a coherent set of principles for
support and regulation, not a single administrative point

of contact.

That said, the location of the VSU in the Home Office seems particularly odd as it is the department most closely identified with control, authority and containment, rather than with enabling. Perhaps we could do no worse than to send the VSU back whence it came, to the Cabinet Office, and give to other departments new duties: for example the Department of the Environment to further develop local strategic initiatives; the Department of Education to integrate community service into schools; the Treasury to encourage innovation in financial mechanisms and better indicators to judge the effectiveness of funding.

The point is that government has as much of a role in setting a climate that should run through all departments as it does in the details of policy mechanisms. If government took seriously the idea of mutual responsibilities; if it much more actively promoted volunteering and community service not only as part of secondary education, but also around work, life and universities; if it overtly valued an independent and often critical set of organisations beyond business and the public sector it would be well-placed to influence a shift in behaviour towards much greater engagement in the community.

To symbolise a new relationship with the voluntary sector the time is probably ripe for a summit to bring together the main institutions concerned with voluntary action in business, the public sector, voluntary organisations, as well as donors and beneficiaries, to start mapping out the route to a new settlement. To work such summits require considerable preparation - policy proposals, consultation, identification of best practices and benchmarks. But when done right they mobilise considerable energies for change.

A government that did all of these things would help to set a tone, and to consolidate a culture. But such policies cannot be seen in isolation. There is an indivisibility. If in other actions ethics are ignored, or downplayed; if real power is seen to reside with organised business and organised labour at the expense of community organisations; if lipservice is not followed through with policy energy, then there is likely to be disappointment and disillusion. Moreover if political leaders themselves do not demonstrate balanced lives, in which they give to others as well as to their own careers, it will be hard for the public to take them seriously.

Recommend- ations

A far-reaching new settlement is now needed to provide the basis for voluntary and ethically motivated action in the next century. In this report we have set out some of the elements, recommending:

● A simplified set of core legal principles from which organisations should be able to choose - balancing incentives for participants, liability and risk-taking, and accountability. These should be developed to replace the cumbersome and anachronistic legal forms, with often unlimited liability, through which most voluntary activity now has to operate.
● The development of new models of public funding, involving a partnership between government and charities, linked to more sophisticated measures of success, including subjective and qualitative indicators that involve the public in their definition.
● Tax benefits to be given to activities commonly defined as public goods rather than specific organizational forms such as charities. This would enable a rationalisation of tax incentives to better fit the most pressing social needs.
● New financial mechanisms to direct money to social

goals: in particular a system of voluntary taxation using the Inland Revenue for taxpayers to earmark money to charitable activity, focusing initially on income tax and Council Tax.

● New support for charitable investments, loans, bonds and guarantees (including a Charitable Investment Scheme and a Charity Enterprise Zone); and a new set of institutions including a Charity Bank, all to provide new outlets for individual generosity.

● Removing the remaining restrictions on free speech for charities, to enable them to play a full part in political life and allow the public to determine whether this is acceptable.

● An 'Investors in the Community' kitemark for companies involved in community activities, so as to promote responsible business involvement in community activities.

● A new CONNECT scheme for community service, for the unemployed and others, to promote volunteering and encourage new links between self-interest and the wider interest of the community.

● A shift in public funding to deliberately encourage innovation and experiment, with a fixed proportion of funding for the voluntary sector (initially 0.5%) for risk funding.

● A rethink across government of its relationship to voluntary organisations, avoiding a single point of contact which is no longer viable for such a wide range of activities.

● A high profile summit, bringing together the key actors and hosted by government, to take forward the work of this report, the NCVO Commission, the work of the political parties, and ensuring the full participation of donors and beneficiaries, to map out the route to a new settlement.

Suppose all of these recommendations were enacted. How would life be different? Most of the elements we have described would have incremental but cumulative effects.

They would steadily work through the culture and the political system, both at a national and a local level. They would shape the workings of business and change the ways in which the voluntary world sees itself.

The benefits from going down the roads we have suggested would be many. Some would be about mood: a greater pride in engagement, a greater confidence about helping others and generosity. Some would be very practical - significant new resources to meet social goals, raised through new investment mechanisms as well as voluntary taxation. There would be new options for the unemployed to become active - not as an answer to unemployment but as a significant amelioration of it. There would be a more outward looking, internationalist voluntary sector, and a further shift in business culture towards engagement with the communities in which it works. There would be a greater valuing of responsibility and connection. And, perhaps most of all, we might achieve a society more comfortable with its own ethics and more energised to solve its own problems.

Notes

1.These figures are drawn from the Henley Centre, Local Futures, 1994

2 James Q. Wilson, The Moral Sense, The Free Press, 1993

3. Such ideas run counter to a very important strand of Western thought which has believed in the hegemony of culture and, thus, in the capacity of people to choose their own values.

4. Robert Wright, The Moral Animal, Pantheon Books, 1994

5.Leda Cosmides, Evolutionary Psychology and the generation of culture, Ethology and Sociobiology, 10, 1987. See also David Erdal and Andrew Whiten 'On Human Egalitarianism: an evolutionary product of Machiavellian status escalation' in Current Anthropology, April 1994.

6. James Q. Wilson, op cit

7. Ibid

8. Clearly many issues arise from this set of arguments. One is how to balance the moral senses with the others - particularly male aggression which rises when gender roles are less clear, and which has become the source of many of the problems which voluntary organisations are asked to help resolve (and it is interesting to note that males are more active in activities to do with children's education and schools or health and social welfare.) A second issue concerns the family. Helping and sharing behaviour is more generally found in families, friendship networks and kinship groups. It is stronger in smaller communities than larger ones,

stronger in rural areas than in urban settings.

9. See Albert Hirschman, Shifting Involvements, Princeton University Press, 1982. The same was true of such phrases as 'felicita publica' or 'bonheur publique'.

10 Crucially many experiments have shown that happy people are more helpful, generous and altruistic. These effects are far from trivial. In one experiment 47% of subjects, who had been put in a good mood by recalling past events, offered to give blood, against 17% in a control group. Another study comparing happy and less happy people against selfishness came up with the following conclusion: 41.6% of the happy group were willing to act unselfishly against 17.5% of the less happy group. (See Michael Argyle, The Psychology of Happiness, Routledge, London, 1987.)

11. Jose Harris, Private Lives, Public Spirit: Britain 1870-1915, Penguin 1994 p.250

12. Frank Prochaska, The Voluntary Impulse, Chatto, 1988

13. Raymond Williams, Keywords, Fontana, 1978

14. See the various studies undertaken by Diana Leat including Challenging Management, JRF, 1995

15. Jeremy Kendall and Martin Knapp, Voluntary Means, Social Ends, Draft January 1995

16. Michael Fogarty and Ian Christie, Companies and Communities, PSI, 1991.

17. Russell Sparkes, The Ethical Investor, Harper Collins 1995, and The Money Game, Demos, 1995, p9

18. The Time Squeeze, Demos Quarterly No. 5, 1995

19. Salamon and Anheier, The Emerging Sector: New Findings, The John Hopkins University Press, Baltimore, 1994.

20. According to the statistics gathered by the Volunteer Centre in 1991, over half the population has volunteered. If these figures are turned into hours they represent circa 62,000,000 hours of formal volunteering a week, such as being a committee member or secretary of a voluntary group and 40,000,000 hours of informal volunteering, such as visiting elderly or sick people or driving people around. In total, these amount to around 100,000,000 hours a week or 5,000,000,000 hours a year. To appreciate the enormity of this voluntary effort, it is interesting to translate this into its full time annual equivalent of 600,000 jobs. Nearly two thirds of voluntary activity involved raising or handling money; about half were involved in organising an event or activity, and about a quarter serve on a committee or provide transport. The most common forms of volunteering involve sports and exercise, children's education, health and social welfare.Over three quarters of people give at least something to charity each month whether in the form of prompted donations in response to appeals (33%), street collections (28%). 26% sponsored someone in an event. Planned giving, such as through the Gift Aid Scheme, payroll giving or covenants, represent only 12%. Overall the average level of donation is £11 per month, although as this also averages in the large donations £3 is a more realistic median.

21.The Volunteer Centre, Who Volunteers and Why?, 1994

22. Ibid

23. Richard Sternberg, 1990, Taxes and giving: new findings, Volunteer, vol 2 no. 2, 61-79. Andrew M. Jones and John W. Posnett, 1993, 'The economics of charity', in Nicholas Barr and David Whynes, (eds) Current Issues in the Economics of Welfare MacMillan, Basingstoke, 1993 pp130-152.

24. Across the Geographical Divide, Centre for Innovation in Voluntary Action, 1995

25.This was recommended amongst others by Mai Wan in

Building Social Capital (IPPR), 1994

26. See In Whose Service: making community service work for the unemployed by Ivan Briscoe, Demos, 1995

27.In Albert Hirschman, Shifting Involvements, p.87

28.This was the conclusion of a pilot study in Coventry on 'Resourcing the Local Voluntary Sector' by Julia Unwin and Peter Westland (1995). The study also highlighted the absence of any coordination between different public sector funders.

29. Friedrich Hayek, Law Legislation and Liberty: a new statement of the liberal priciples of justice and political economy, Routledge, 1982.

30. Mancur Olson, The Rise and Fall of Nations, Yale University Press, 1982.

31. Friedrich Hayek, op cit.

32. John Stuart Mill, On Liberty, Cambridge University Press, 1989.

33. James Madison, A. Hamilton and John Jay, Federalist Papers, Penguin Classics, 1987

34. Perri 6, Restricting the Freedom of Speech of Charities: do the rationales stand up? Paper No. 6, Demos, 1994. Also in Perri 6 and Anita Randon, Liberty, Charity and Politcs: non-profit law and freedom of speech, Dartmouth, Aldershot, 1995

35. Quoted in Lester Salamon, The Global Associational Revolution: The rise of the third sector on the world scene, Demos, 1995.

36. Ibid

37. Ibid

38. Charities and Trading; a recent report, KPMG Peat Marwick, 1994.

39 This is one of the justifications in Barry Bracewell-Milnes, 'The Wealth of Giving', IEA, 1989

40 Steinberg, 1990; Jones and Posnett, 1993; Jones and Marriott and associates, 1994

41. This is the criterion of 'treasury efficiency'; technically, the requirement is that the negative slope of the curve describing the elasticity of change in charitable giving in response to marginal changes, as a result of marginal changes in tax relief or the rate of tax, in the efficiency price - the price not merely of increasing the charity's income by one pound, but the price of increasing its output by one pound's worth of giving, should be greater than minus one. See Steinberg, 1990, Jones and Marriott and associates, 1994 and 6, 1993d for a discussion of the criterion.

42 Russell Sparkes, The Money Game, Demos, 1995.

43. Geoff Mulgan, Reconnecting Taxation, Demos, 1993

44. John Griffiths, The Acceptable Face of Capitalism, Demos, 1994.

Bibliography

Albery and Mezey (eds.) (1994) Reinventing Society - A Bumper Book of Best Ideas, Schemes and Speculations, Institute for Social Inventions.

Alfandari, E., and Nardone, A., (eds.) (1990), Les associations et les fondations en Europe: regime juridique et fiscal , editions Juris Service, Lyon.

Anheier, H.K., and Seibel, W., (eds.) (1990), The third sector: comparative studies of nonprofit organisations , de Gruyter, Berlin and New York.

Argyle, M. (1987) The Psychology of Happiness, Routledge, London and New York.

Argyle, M. (1991) Cooperation - The Basis of Sociability. Routledge, London and New York.

Atkinson, R. (1994) The Common Sense of Community, Demos, London

Avineri, S and Avner de S (eds) (1992) Communitarianism and Individualism, Oxford University Press.

Badelt, C., (1992), 'Voluntary organisations in the welfare state: equity versus efficiency issues in institutional choice', paper given at the Third international conference of research on voluntary and non-profit organisations , Indianapolis, Indiana, USA, March 11-13, 1992.

Batsleer, J, Cornforth, C. and Paton, R. (1991), Issues in Voluntary and Non-Profit Management, Addison-Wesley, Wokingham

Ben-Ner, A., and van Hoomissen, T., (1991), 'Nonprofit

organisations in the mixed economy: a demand and supply analysis', Annals of public and co-operative economics , vol. 62, no. 4, 519-550.

Bennett, J.T., and DiLorenzo, T.J., (1989), Unfair competition: the profit of nonprofits , Hamilton Press, Lanham, Maryland

Beresford, P., and Croft, S. (1993) Citizen Involvement - A practical guide for change, Macmillan, Basingstoke.

Berle, A., and Means, G., (1932), The modern corporation and private property , MacMillan, New York.

Blacksell, S. and Phillips, D. R. (1994), Voluntary Action Research, Third Series Paper 2, Paid to Volunteer. The Volunteer Centre UK.

Boswell, J. (1994) Community and the Economy: The theory of public co-operation, Routledge, London

Carter, N., Klein, R., and Day, P., (1992), How organisations measure success: the use of performance indicators in government, Routledge, London.

Charities Aid Foundation (various years), Charity trends , Charities Aid Foundation, London and Tonbridge.

Clotfelter, C.T., (ed.) (1992), Who benefits from the nonprofit sector? , University of Chicago Press, Chicago.

Cowan, T., (1993), 'Altruism and the argument from offsettting transfers', in Paul, E.F., Miller, F.D., and Paul, J., (eds.) (1993), Altruism , Cambridge University Press, 225-246. (also published as a special issue of Social philosophy and policy , vol. 10, no.1).den Uyl, D.J., (1993), 'The right to welfare and the virtue of charity', in Paul, E.F., Miller, F.D., and Paul, J., (eds.) (1993), Altruism , Cambridge University Press, 192-224. (also published as a special issue of Social philosophy and policy , vol. 10, no.1).

Csikszentmihalyi, M. (1992), Flow - The Psychology of Happiness, Rider.

DiMaggio, P., and Powell, W. W., (1983), 'The iron cage revisited: institutional isomorphism and collective rationality in organisational fields', American Sociological Review , 48, 147-60; revised and reprinted in Powell and DiMaggio (eds.) (19); pp. 63-82.

Drucker, H. (1993) Post-Capitalist Society, Butterworth Heinemann, Oxford

Dunleavy, P., (19), Democracy, bureaucracy and public choice , Harvester Wheatsheaf, Hemel Hempstead.

Eckel, C., and Steinberg, R., (1993a), 'Competition, performance and public policy toward nonprofits', in Hammack, D., and Young, D.R., (eds.) (1993), Nonprofit organisations in a market economy , Jossey-Bass, San Francisco.

Eckel, C., and Steinberg, R., (1993b), 'Tax policy and the objectives of nonprofit organisations', mimeo, Dept. of Economics, Indiana University - Purdue University, Indianapolis.

Etzioni, A. (1993), The Parenting Deficit, Demos, LondonGaul, G., and Borowski, N., (1993), Free ride: the tax-exempt economy , Andrews and McNeel, Kansas City.Gidron, B., Kramer, R.M., and Salamon, L.M., (eds.) (1992), Government and the third sector: emerging relationships in welfare states , Jossey-Bass, San Francisco.

Goodin, R.E., (1985), Protecting the vulnerable: a re-analysis of our social responsibilities , University of Chicago Press, Chicago

Green, D.G., (1993), Reinventing civil society: the rediscovery of welfare without politics , Choice in welfare series no.17, Institute of Economic Affairs Health and Welfare Unit, London.

Gronbjerg, K.A., (1993), Understanding nonprofit funding: managing revenues in social services and community development organisations , Jossey-Bass, San Francisco.

Gutch, R. (1992), Contracting Lessons from the US, NCV PublicationsHall, P.D., (1992a), Inventing the nonprofit sector and other essays in philanthropy, voluntarism and nonprofit organisations , Johns Hopkins University Press, Baltimore.

Hall, P.D., (1992b), 'Reflections on the nonprofit sector in the postliberal era', in Hall (1992a) 85-115.

Hansmann, H.B., (1980), 'The role of nonprofit enterprise', Yale law review , April 190: 835-98; reprinted in Rose-Ackerman (ed) (1986), 57-84.

Hansmann, H.B., (1981), 'The rationale for exempting nonprofit organisations from corporate income taxation', Yale law journal , :54-100; reprinted in Rose-Ackerman (ed.) (1986) 367-393.

Harvey, D., (1989), The Urban Experience, Blackwell, Oxford

Hawley, K., (1992), From grants to contracts: a practical guide for voluntary organisations , NCVO and Directory of Social Change, London.

Hayek, F.A., (1977-82), Law, legislation and liberty: a new statement of the liberal principles of justice and political economy , three vols, Routledge and Kegan Paul, London.

Hazell, R. (ed) (1993) Resourcing the Voluntary Sector. The Funders' Perspective. Association of Chari o Foundations, London

Hirst, P.Q., (1993), Associative democracy , Verso, London.

Hodgkinson, V.A., Weitzman, M.S., Toppe, C.M., and Noga, S.M., (1992), Nonprofit almanac 1992-3: dimensions of the independent sector , Jossey-Bass, San Francisco and Independent Sector, Washington D.C.

Isaac, A. J. G.,(1992), Local Income Tax. A Study of the Options, Joseph Rowntree Foundation.

Jackson, T. and Marks, N. (1994) Stockholm Environment Institute, Measuring Sustainable Economic Welfare, A Pilot Index, 19950 - 1990, Stockholm Environment Institute.

James, E., (ed.) (1989), The nonprofit sector in international perspective: studies in comparative culture and policy , Oxford University Press, New York.

Jones, A.M., and Marriott, R., and associates, 'The economics of chari o giving and taxation policy', paper given at the Non-Profit Studies and Demos symposium, The economics of voluntary action , School for Advanced Urban Studies, University of Bristol, 13.4.94.

Jones, A.M., and Posnett, J.W., (1993), 'The economics of charity'', in Barr, N., and Whynes, D., (eds.) (1993), Current issues in the economics of welfare , MacMillan, Basingstoke, 130-152.

Kendall, J., and 6, P., (1994), 'Government and the voluntary sector in the United Kingdom', in Saxon-Harrold, S.K.E., and Kendall, J., (eds.) (1994), Researching the voluntary sector, 2nd series , Charities Aid Foundation, Tonbridge and London: 16-40.

Kendall, J. and Knapp, M.. (1995), Voluntary Means, Socila Ends. Policy Issues for the UK Voluntary Sector in the 1990s.

Korten, D. C., (1990), Getting to the 21st Century - Voluntary Action and the Global Agenda, Kumarian Press, Connecticut, USA

Knapp, M.R.J., (1984), The economics of social care , MacMillan, Basingstoke.

Knapp, M.R.J., (1988), 'Private and voluntary welfare', in Sullivan,

Bibliography

M., (ed.) (1988), The new politics of welfare , MacMillan, Basingstoke.Knight, B., (1993), Voluntary Action, Centris, London.Kramer, R.M., and Grossman, B., (1987), 'Contracting for social services: process management and resource dependencies', Social services review , March, 32-55.

Kuhnle, S., and Selle, P., (eds.) (1992), Government and voluntary organisations: a relational perspective , Avebury, Aldershot.

Laville, J-L, (1994), L'economie solidaire: une perspective internationale, Desclee de Brouwer, Paris

Leat, D., (1992), Trusts in transition: the policy and practice of grant-giving trusts , Joseph Rowntree Foundation, York.

Leat, D., (1993), Managing across sectors: similarities and differences between for-profit and voluntary non-profit organisations , Centre for Voluntary Sector and Not-for-Profit Management, The Business School, City University, London.

Leat, D., Tester, S., and Unell, J., (1986), A price worth paying? A study of the effects of government grant aid to voluntary organisations ,

Policy Studies Institute, London.

O Grand, J., and Bartlett, W., (eds.) (1993), Quasi-markets and social policy , MacMillan, Basingstoke.Lloyd, T., (1993) The Charity Business: The New Philanthropists, John Murray.

Lynn, P., (19), Voluntary Action Research. Second Series Paper No.1., SCRR.McQillan, J., (1992), 15th Edition. Charity Trends 1992, Charities Aid Foundation, KentMcQillan, J., (1993), 16th Edition. Charity Trends 1993, Charities Aid Foundation, Kent

Maslow, A. H., (1954), Motivation and Personality, Harper Collins, London

Melucci, A. (19), Il gioco dell'io. Il cambiamento di se in una societa globale, Saggi/Feltrinelli

Middleton, F., and Lloyd, S., (1992), Charities: the new law: the Charities Act 1992 , Jordans, Bristol.

Miller, G., (1992), Managerial dilemmas: the political economy of hierarchy , Cambridge University Press.

Milofsky, C., (1987), 'Neighbourhood-based organisations: a market analogy', in Powell, (ed.) (1987), 277-295.

Morgan, G. (1986), Images of Organisation, Sage

Publications.

Olson, M., (1971), The logic of collective action: public goods and the theory of groups , Harvard University Press, Cambridge, Massachusetts and London.

Osborne, S.P., (1993), 'The role of voluntary organisations in innovation in social welfare services', paper given at the conference, Well-being in Europe by strengthening the third sector , Barcelona, 27-29.5.93.

Owen, D., (1964), English philanthropy 1660-1960 , Harvard University Press, Cambridge, Massachusetts.

Powell, W.W., (ed.), (1987), The nonprofit sector: a research handbook , Yale University Press, New Haven.Prochaska, F., (1988), The voluntary impulse: philanthropy in modern Britain , Faber and Faber, London.

Proschaska, F. (1988) The Voluntary Impulse, Chatto and Windus, London.

Rawls, J., (1971), A theory of justice , Oxford University Press.Rawls, J., (1993), Political liberalism , Columbia University Press, New York.

Room, G., and 6, P., (1994), 'Welfare states in Europe and the third sector', in 6 and Vidal (eds.) (1994).

Rose-Ackerman, S., (ed.) (1986), The economics of nonprofit institutions: studies in structure and policy , Oxford University Press, New York.

Rose-Ackerman, S., (1990), 'Competition between non-profits and for-profits: entry and growth', Voluntas , vol. 1, no. 1, 13-25.

Rowntree Foundation, Joseph (1994), Saving for Credit - the future for credit unions in Britain, National Consumer Council.

Salamon, L.M., (1993), The nonprofit sector: a primer , Foundation Center, New York.

Salamon, L.M., and Anheier, H.K., (1992a), 'In search of the nonprofit sector I: the question of definition', Voluntas , vol. 3, no. 2, 125-152.

Salamon, L.M., and Anheier, H.K., (1992b), 'In search of the nonprofit sector II: the problem of classification', Voluntas , vol. 3, no. 3, 267-310.

Saxon-Harrold, S. K. E. (ed) (1994), 2nd edition. Researching the Voluntary Sector. A National, Local and International Perspective, Charities Aid Foundation, Kent.

Saxon-Harrold, S. K. E., (ed) (1993), 1st edition. Researching the Voluntary Sector. Charities Aid

Foundation.Schiff, J., and Weisbrod, B.A., (19), 'Competition between for-profit and nonprofit organisations in commercial activities', Annals of public and co-operative economics , vol. 62, no. 4, 619-640.

Schuster, J.M.D., (1989), 'Government leverage of private support: matching grants and the problem with 'new' money', paper given at the ALA Arts research seminar, The costs of culture : proceedings, 63-97.

Selbourne, D. (1993), The Spirit of the Age - an account of our times,

Selznick, P. (1994) The Moral Commonwelath: social theory and the promise of community, University of California Press, Berkeley.

Sinclair-StevensonSheridan, L.A., and Keeton, G., (1993), The modern law of charities , 4th edn., University College Cardiff Press.

Singer, P. (1994) How Are We To Live? Ethics in an age of self-interest, Mandarin, London.

Smith, S.R., and Lipsky, M., (1993), Nonprofits for hire: the welfare state in the age of contracting , Harvard University Press, Cambridge, Massachusetts.

Sousi, G., and Mayaud., Y., (eds.) (1992), O droit des associations: vol. 1: Belgique, France, Italie, Luxembourg, Pays-Bas, Statut de l'Association Europeane , Commission of the European Communities in association with editions Lamy, Brussels.

Sparkes, R. (1995), The Ethical Investor - How to make money work for society and the environment as well as for yourself, Harper Collins

Steinberg, R., (1990), 'Taxes and giving: new findings', Voluntas, vol. 1, no. 2, 61-79.

Steinberg, R., (19b), ''Unfair' competition by nonprofits and tax policy', National tax journal , vol. 44, 351-364.

Steinberg, R., (1993a), 'Public policy and the performance of nonprofit organisations: a general framework', Nonprofit and voluntary sector quarterly, vol. 22, no. 1, 13-32.

Steinberg, R., (1993b), 'How should antitrust laws apply to nonprofit organisations?', in Young, D.R., Hollister, R., Hodgkinson, V., and associates (eds.) (1992), Governing, leading and managing nonprofit organisations: new insights from research and practice , Jossey-Bass, San Francisco, 279-305.

Steinberg, R., (1993c), 'Competition policy and contracted markets', paper given at the NCVO - South Bank University conference, Contracting - selling or shrinking? , 20-22.7.93, London.

Taylor, M., and Hoggett, P., (1994), 'Trusting in networks? the third sector and welfare change', in 6 and Vidal (eds.) (1994).

Taylor, M., Langan, J., and Hoggett, P., (1994), 'Independent organisations in community care', in Saxon-Harrold, S.K.E., and Kendall, J., (eds.) (1994), Researching the voluntary sector, 2nd series , Charities Aid Foundation, Tonbridge and London: 129-151

Thake, S. and Staubach R, (1993), Investing in People - rescuing communities from the margin. Joseph Rowntree Foundation, York.

Thomas, A. and Finch, H. (1990), Voluntary Action Research Paper No. 2, On Volunteering: A Qualititative Research Study of Images, Motivations and Experiences, Social and Community Planning Research.

Wann, M. (1995), Building Social Capital. Self-help in a twenty-first century welfare state. Institute for Public Policy Research.

Weisbrod, B.A., and Schlesinger, M., (1986), 'Public, private, nonprofit ownership and the response to asymmetric information: the case of nursing homes', in Rose-Ackerman, (ed.) (1986), 133-151.

Williams, I., (1989), The alms trade: charities, past, present and future , Unwin Hyman, London.

Williams, H. S. and Webb, A. Y., (1992), Outcome Funding. A New Approach to Public Sector Grant-Making, The Rensselaerville Institute, New York.

Wilson, J. Q., (1993), The Moral Sense, The Free Press, New YorkWolpert, J., (1993), Patterns of generosity in America: who's holding the safety net? , Twentieth Century Fund Press, New York.

Woltenden Committee, Report of, 1978. The Future of Voluntary Organisations, Croom Helm, London.

Wright, R. (1994), The Moral Animal. Why we are the way we are: the new science of Evolutionary Psychology. Pantheon Books, New York.

6, P., (19),   What is a voluntary organisation? Defining the voluntary and nonprofit sectors , National Council for Voluntary Organisations, London.

6, P., (1992), 'European competition law and the non-profit sector', Voluntas , vol. 3, no. 2, 215-246.

6, P., (1993a), 'Foundations: cross-national policy issues', paper given at the Voluntas symposium, Foundations: an international research symposium , October 22-24, 1993, Paris.

6, P., (1993b), 'Innovation by nonprofit organisations: policy and research issues', Nonprofit management and leadership , vol. 3, no.4, 397-414.

6, P., (1993c), 'The co-ordination problem and institutions in non-profit studies: a research agenda', paper given at the conference, Well-being in Europe by strengthening the third sector , Barcelona, 27-29.5.93.6, P., (1993d), 'Taxation policy and non-profit bodies in Europe', Social services research , 1993, no.2, 5-21.

6, P., (1994a; in press), 'The voluntary and non-profit sectors in continental Europe', in Davis Smith, J., Hedley, R., and Rochester, R., (eds.) (1994), An introduction to the voluntary sector , Routledge.

6, P., and Kuti, E., (1993), 'Into the European Community: impacts of future membership on Hungary's non-profit sector', Journal of European Social Policy , vol. 3, no. 4, 273-296.

6, P., and Randon, A., (1995), Liberty, charity and politics , Dartmouth Publishing Ltd, Aldershot.

6, P., and Vidal, I., (eds.) (1994), Delivering welfare: re-positioning non-profit and co-operative action in western European welfare states , Centre for Initiatives in the Social Economy, University of Barcelona, Barcelona.

Charity Project Working Papers -

No. 1 *Themes and Issues* - Charles
   Landry and Geoff Mulgan
   ISBN 1 898309 65 5
No. 2 *Rethinking Charity Finance* -
   Geoff Mulgan and Charles
   Landry
   ISBN 1 898309 50 7
No. 3 *The Question of Independence* -
   Perri 6
   ISBN 1 898309 60 4
No. 4 *The Future of Civic Forms of
   Organisation* - Paul Hoggett
   ISBN 1 898309 55 8
No. 5 *The Acceptable Face of
   Capitalism?* - John Griffiths
   ISBN 1 898309 85 X
No. 6 *Restricting the Freedom of
   Speech of Charities* - Perri 6
   ISBN 1 898309 90 6
No. 7 *The Global Associational
   Revolution* - Lester Salamon
   ISBN 1 898309 36 1
No. 8 *The Money Game: Money,
   Charities and the City* - Russell
   Sparkes
   ISBN 1 898309 51 5

*In Whose Service? Making community
service work for the unemployed* by
Ivan Briscoe is also available.

All these papers cost £5 each or
£30 for the complete set.